THE MAGIC OF WINE

THE MAGIC OF

Wine

JACQUELINE L. QUILLEN

AND

GEORGE H. BOYNTON SR.

TAYLOR PUBLISHING COMPANY

DALLAS, TEXAS

Designed by Barbara Werden
Set in Adobe Minion

Published by Taylor Publishing Company
1550 West Mockingbird Lane
Dallas, Texas 75235
www.taylorpub.com

LIBRARY OF CONGRESS CATALOGING-IN-PUBLICATION DATA

The magic of wine/[compiled] by Jacqueline L. Quillen and George H. Boynton Sr.
   p. cm.
  ISBN 0-87833-173-5
  1. Wine—Quotations, maxims, etc. I. Quillen, Jacqueline L. II. Boynton, George H.

PN6084.W5 M34 2000
641.2'2—dc21   99-055747

10 9 8 7 6 5 4 3 2 1

PRINTED IN THE UNITED STATES OF AMERICA

TO TIMOTHY COLTMAN-ROGERS

Then I commended mirth, because a man hath no better thing under the sun, than to eat, and to drink, and to be merry: for that shall abide with him of his labor the days of his life, which God giveth him under the sun.

ECCLES. 8:15

CONTENTS

INTRODUCTION

*. . . wine is more than a mere beverage . . .
it is one of the indices of civilization
and, therefore, worthy of life study.*

CLIFTON FADIMAN

WINE historically connects us to ancient civilizations, geographically to distant parts of the globe, and spiritually to the myths and beliefs that form our culture. *The Epic of Gilgamesh* (2000 B.C.) is the earliest known work of literature which discusses wine. It relates how a hero, Gilgamesh, journeying in search of immortal life, visits the land of the sun, a paradise in which he finds a vineyard where "grape-vine was trellised, good to behold." Its keeper was a divine being, a woman who dispensed the "noble and precious fluid" made from the vineyard and which conferred immortality. However, Gilgamesh did not achieve immortality; he had to travel on.

As *The Epic of Gilgamesh* indicates, wine is interwoven with the very beginnings of human history. Textiles, pottery, and bread can be traced back to the Stone Age, but wine alone has a diversity of uses that gives it a life of its own. In addition to being a liquid food for over 8,000 years, only wine was charged with religious sacramental meaning, as well as healing powers. The idea of libation—pouring wine upon the ground as a gift to the gods—is connected with the earliest religious rituals.

Wine has certain properties that mattered much more to our ancestors than to ourselves. For 2,000 years of medical and surgical history, it was the universal and unique antiseptic. Wounds were bathed with it, and water made safe to drink.

In Christianity, wine is the supreme symbol of unity between the human and the divine as embodied in communion. There are more than 150 references to wine in *The Old Testament*. The importance of wine to the people is poignantly illustrated in *Isaiah*:

> *There is a crying for wine in the streets; all*
> *joy is darkened, the mirth of the land is gone.*

Even the austere St. Paul recognized the significance of wine in *I Timothy*:

> *Drink no longer water, but use a little wine for thy*
> *stomach's sake and thine other infirmities.*

Wine has been praised for centuries by statesmen, scholars, poets, and philosophers. Socrates recognized the beneficial effects of wine:

> *Wine moistens and tempers the spirits, and lulls the cares*
> *of the mind to rest. . . . It revives our joys, and is oil to the*
> *dying flame of life. If we drink temperately, and small*
> *draughts at a time, the wine distills into our lungs like*
> *sweetest morning dew. . . . It is then the wine commits no*
> *rape upon our reason, but pleasantly invites us to agreeable*
> *mirth.*

Some people dread all external stimuli. They regard wine as a danger. For those to whom wine brings no inspiration, no moment of sudden illumination of wider and deeper insight of larger human charity and understanding, it will be difficult to realize what to those of a different temperament is natural and beautiful—the constant shift from physical to spiritual that is the essence of the religion of Dionysus.

Wine is an intimate part of religion, history, myth, literature, science, and art. Wine serves as a festive drink at birth, a solemn drink at death, a sacred drink in religious ceremonies, and a stimulant for discussion from dinner parties to symposia. The moment wine is added, the tone is changed. The influence becomes one of learning. The learning may be practical—the making and selling of wine embraces botany, chemistry, agriculture, economics—all of this constitutes part of the pleasure of wine, but such mundane considerations played little part in the compilation of this book. Our motivation was the aesthetic enjoyment one feels when sharing good wine with good friends. As Ernest Hemingway noted, wine can also be a companion and alleviate solitude:

> *I drank a bottle of wine for company. It was a Chateau Margaux. It was pleasant to be drinking slowly and to be tasting the wine and to be drinking alone. A bottle of wine was good company.*

For most of us, the stimulations and satisfactions of wine are within the bottle. The whole process of living can be enriched by the miracle that is in wine. The unique diversity of wines represents a broad range of possible sensations. Pulling corks enhances conviviality and binds individuals together; we have yet to discover a selfish wine lover. Wine begs to be shared, and we should like to share with you, in this book, some of the fun and enjoyment wine has given to us.

Pleasures of Wine

And wine maketh glad the heart of man.

PSALMS 104:15

Wine has the most precious quality that art has; it makes ideas, people, incidents, places, sensations seem larger than life.

HUGH JOHNSON

Wine is alive, and when you offer it to your fellow man, you are offering him life. More than that, you are calling out more life in him, you are engaging in what might be called a creative flattery, for you are asking him to summon up his powers of discrimination, to exercise his taste, or perhaps merely to evince curiosity or a desire to learn.

CLIFTON FADIMAN

I can no more think of my own life without thinking of wine and wines and where they grew for me and why I drank them when I did and why I picked the grapes and where I opened the oldest procurable bottles, and all that, than I can remember living before I breathed. In other words, wine is life, and my life and wine are inextricable. And the saving grace of all wine's many graces, probably, is that it can never be dull. It is only the people who try to sing about it who may sound flat. But wine is an older thing than we are, and is forgiving of even the most boring explanation of its *elan vital.*

M. F. K. FISHER

The joy that is in Wine is the joy of sunshine. . . . Wine is not a drug. It is never a craving. It seldom becomes even a mere habit. It is an instinct, a man's time-honoured urge to joy.

ANDRE L. SIMON

O, for a draught of vintage!
    That hath been
Cool'd a long age in the deep-
    delved earth,
Tasting of Flora and the country
    green,
Dance, and Provencal song, the
    sunburnt mirth!
O for a beaker full of the warm
    South,
Full of the true, the blushful
    Hippocrene,
With beaded bubbles winking at
    the brim,
And purple-stained mouth;
That I might drink and leave
    the world unseen,

And with thee fade away into
   the forest dim.

JOHN KEATS

When I am asked, as I sometimes am, what is the bottle of
wine I have most enjoyed, I have
to answer that it was probably
some anonymous Italian fiasco
that I drank one starlit
Tyrrhenian night under a vine-
covered arbour, while a
Neapolitan fiddler played
"Come Back to Sorrento" over
the veal cutlet of the young
woman I had designs on. . . .
 For not only is taste in wine as
subjective as taste in women,
but its enjoyment depends more
on circumstances than does that
of almost any other pleasure.

CYRIL RAY

Few things surpass old wine;
   and
 they may preach
Who please, the more because
   they
 preach in vain,—

Let us have wine and women,
   mirth
 and laughter,

Sermons and soda-water the day
   after.

GEORGE GORDON, LORD
BYRON

A Book of Verses underneath
   the Bough,
A Jug of Wine, a Loaf of
   Bread—and Thou
Beside me singing in the
   Wilderness—
Oh, Wilderness were Paradise
   enow.

OMAR KHAYYÁM

No draught of wine amid the
old tombs under the violet sky
but made me for the time a
better man, larger of brain,
more courageous, more gentle.
'Twas a revelry whereon came
no repentance. Could I but live
forever in thoughts and feelings
such as those born to me in the
shadow of the Italian vine!

GEORGE GISSING

I sat in a large airy café, listening to sentimental music, sipping a sweet sparkling wine, realizing how wine could not only wash away one's cares but heighten one's big moments.

ALEC WAUGH

I drank at every vine
    The last was like the first.
I came upon no wine
    So wonderful as thirst.

EDNA ST. VINCENT MILLAY

Wine makes every meal an occasion, every table more elegant, every day more civilized.

ANDRE L. SIMON

Wine, it's in my veins, and I can't get it out.

BURGESS MEREDITH

The dew is heavy on the grass,
At last the sun is set.
Fill up, fill up the cup of jade,
The night's before us yet.

CHINESE POEM

All wines are by their very nature full of reminiscence, the golden tears and red blood of summers that are gone.

RICHARD LE GALLIENNE

The point of drinking wine is to get in touch with one of the major influences of western civilization, to taste sunlight trapped in a bottle, and to remember some stony slopes in Tuscany or a village by the Gironde.

JOHN MORTIMER

How great a thing is a single
    cup of wine!
For it makes us tell the story of
    our whole lives.

PO CHU-I

Wine can of their wits the wise
    beguile,
Make the sage frolic, and the
    serious smile.

HOMER

Our pale day is sinking into
    twilight.
And if we sip the wine, we find
    dreams coming upon us out
    of the imminent night.

D. H. LAWRENCE

Perplexed no more with Human
or Divine,
To-morrow's tangle to the winds
re-sign,
And lose your fingers in the
tresses of
The Cypress-slender Minister of
Wine.

OMAR KHAYYÁM

With me I had a goatskin full of
dark fragrant wine, given me by
Maron, Euanthes' son . . .
unmixed and fragrant, a drink
for the gods. . . . He would pour
just one cupful of it into twenty
measures of spring-water; from
the mixing-bowl there would be
wafted a fragrance beyond all
words, and no one could find it
in his heart to refrain.

HOMER

All the great villainies of history,
from the murder of Abel
onward, have been perpetrated
by sober men, and chiefly by
teetotallers. But all the charming
and beautiful things, from the
Song of Songs to bouillabaisse,
and from the nine Beethoven
symphonies to the martini
cocktail, have been given to
humanity by men who, when
the hour came, turned from tap
water to something with colour
to it, and more in it than mere
oxygen and hydrogen.

H. L. MENCKEN

Wine is exaltation for the
mystic; a sense of unity with the
whole and of belonging for the
disinherited; courage for the
timid; peace for the troubled
spirit; nepenthe for the tortured
soul; aphrodisiac for the lover;
surcease for the pain-wracked
soul; anaesthetic for use in
surgery; gaiety for the
depressed.

DAN STANISLAWSKI

Fill the goblet again! For I never
before
Felt the glow which now gladdens my heart to its core.
Let us drink!—who would not?
Since through life's varied
round,
In the goblet alone no deception
is found.

GEORGE GORDON, LORD
BYRON

Good wine's the gift that God
    has given
To man alone beneath the
    heaven,
Of dance and song the genial
    sire,
Of friendship gay and soft
    desire;
Yet rule it with a tightened rein,
Nor moderate wisdom's rules
    disdain;
For when unchecked there's
    nought runs faster—
A useful slave, but cruel master.

PANYASIS

This is the wine-cellar,
The place for the produce of the
    vine is in it.
One is merry in it.
And the heart of him who goes
    forth from it rejoices.

EGYPTIAN INSCRIPTION

Let misers in garrets lay up their
    gay store
And keep their rich bags to live
    wretchedly poor;
'Tis the cellar alone where true
    fame is renowned,
Her treasure's diffusive, and
    cheers all around.
The gold and the gems but the
    eyes' gaudy toy,

But the Vintner's red juice gives
    health, love and joy.

SONG OF THE VINTNER'S
COMPANY

Riches and poverty, long or
    short life,
By the maker of things are
    proportioned and disposed;
But a cup of wine levels life and
    death
And a thousand things obsti-
    nately hard to prove.

LI PO

What miracle cannot the wine-
cup work? It lifts the load from
anxious hearts.

HORACE

I sell well it is necessarie,
Where that we go, good wyn
    with us carie
For that wol turne rancour and
    disese
T'accord and love, and many a
    wrong apese.

GEOFFREY CHAUCER

When there is plenty of wine,
sorrow and worry take wing.

OVID

Man being reasonable must get
 drunk;
The best of life is but intoxication;
Glory, the grape, love, gold—in
 these are sunk
The hopes of all men and of
 every nation.

GEORGE GORDON, LORD
BYRON

. . . wine is the professor of
taste, the liberator of the spirit,
and the light of intelligence. . . .

PAUL CLAUDEL

If you pay attention to it, a good
wine will always have something
to tell you. What exactly it says
no one can ever completely
understand, of course, and that
is wine's charm and its mystery.

JAMES NORWOOD PRATT

A glass of good wine is a gracious creature and reconciles
poor mortality to itself, and that
is what few things can do.

SIR WALTER SCOTT

Go thy way, eat thy bread with
joy, and drink thy wine with a
merry heart.

ECCLES. 9:7

Bacchus we thank who gave us
 wine
Which warms the blood within
 our veins;
That nectar is itself divine.
The man who drinks not, yet
 attains
By godly grace to human rank
Would be an angel if he drank.

PIERRE MOTIN, OLD FRENCH
DRINKING SONG

If all be true that I do think
There are five reasons we should
 drink;
Good wine—a friend—or being
 dry—
Or least we should be by and
 by—
Or any other reason why.

HENRY ALDRICH

Give me books, fruit, French
wine and fine weather and a
little music out of doors, played
by somebody I do not know.

JOHN KEATS

I drink when I have occasion, and sometimes when I have no occasion.

MIGUEL DE CERVANTES

A waltz and a glass of wine can invite an encore.

JOHANN STRAUSS

On a moonlit night, a morning after a snowfall, or under the cherry blossoms, it adds to our pleasure if, while chatting at our ease, we bring forth the wine cups.

YOSHIDA KENKO

Wine in moderation—not in excess, for that makes men ugly—has a thousand pleasant influences. It brightens the eye, improves the voice, imparts a new vivacity to one's thoughts and conversation.

CHARLES DICKENS

The juice of the grape is the liquid quintessence of concentrated sunbeams.

THOMAS LOVE PEACOCK

This wine is too good for toast-drinking, my dear. You don't want to mix emotions up with a wine like that. You lose the taste.

ERNEST HEMINGWAY

This wine should be eaten, it is too good to be drunk.

JONATHAN SWIFT

It is only the first bottle of wine that is expensive.

FRENCH PROVERB

Give me women, wine and snuff
Until I cry out "hold enough!"
You may do so sans objection
Till the day of resurrection;
For bless my beard they aye
    shall be
My beloved Trinity.

JOHN KEATS

Diogenes was asked what wine he liked best, and he answered as I would have done, "Somebody else's."

MICHÊL DE MONTAIGNE

The wine snob is a product of enthusiasm. His interest in labels, chateaux and years . . . is apt, however, to rob him of pleasure. . . . He frequently deprives himself—as no Frenchman, however wealthy in bottles and knowledge of wine, does—of the simple pleasure of humbly nameless but eminently drinkable French table wines.

JOHN ARLOTT

I can truthfully say that since I reached the age of discretion, I have consistently drunk more than most people would say was good for me. Nor do I regret it. Wine has been to me a firm friend and a wise counsellor. Often wine has shown me matters in their true perspective, and has, as though by the touch of a magic wand, reduced great disasters to small inconveniences.

Wine has lit up for me the pages of literature, and revealed in life romance lurking in the commonplace.

Wine has made me bold but not foolish; has induced me to say silly things but not to do them.

Under its influence, words have often come too easily which had better not have been spoken, and letters have been written which had better not have been sent.

But if such small indiscretions standing in the debit column of wine's account were added up, they would amount to nothing in comparison with the vast accumulation on the credit side.

ALFRED DUFF COOPER

One of the oldest and quietest roads to contentment lies through the conventional trinity of wine, woman and song.

REXFORD GUY TUGWELL

There are two reasons for drinking: one is, when you are thirsty, to cure it; the other, when you are not thirsty, to prevent it.

THOMAS LOVE PEACOCK

I've heard him renounce wine a hundred times a day, but then it has been between as many glasses.

DOUGLAS JERROLD

Wine is a friend, wine is a joy;
and, like sunshine, wine is the
birthright of all.

ANDRE L. SIMON

When the wines were good, they
pleased my senses, cheered my
spirits, improved my moral and
intellectual powers, besides
enabling me to confer the same
benefits on other people.

GEORGE SAINTSBURY

Wine has been part of the
human experience since civilization began. It is the natural
beverage for every celebration:
births, graduations, engage-
ments, weddings. Anniversaries,
promotions, family gatherings,
meetings with friends, and
toasts between governments.

ROBERT MONDAVI

I often wonder what the vintners buy,
Half so precious as the stuff
   they sell.

OMAR KHAYYÁM

O, thou bright wine whose
   purple splendor leaps
And bubbles gaily in this golden
   bowl
Under the lamplight as my
   spirits do.

PERCY BYSSHE SHELLEY

Wine gives great pleasure; and
every pleasure is of itself a good.
It is a good, unless counter
balanced by evil.

SAMUEL JOHNSON

Wine was given us of God, not
that we might be drunken, but
that we might be sober; that we
might be glad, not that we give
ourselves pain.

ST. JOHN CHRYSOSTOM

One not only drinks wine, one
smells it, observes it, tastes it,
sips it, and one talks about it.

KING EDWARD VII

Bacchus, son of Semele
And of Zeus, discovered wine
Giving it to man to be
Care's oblivious anodyne.

ALCAEUS

A feast is made for laughter and
wine maketh merry. . . .

ECCLES. 10:19

Five qualities there are wine's
    praise advancing:
Strong, beautiful, fragrant, cool
    and dancing.

JOHN HARRINGTON

Wine is one of the most civilized things in the world and one of the natural things of the world that has been brought to the greatest perfection, and it offers a greater range of enjoyment and appreciation than, possibly, any other purely sensory thing which may be purchased.

ERNEST HEMINGWAY

The pleasures of wine, being both sensory and intellectual, are profound. There are few pleasures of which this can be said.

CLIFTON FADIMAN

I sometimes think I hear wine talking. It speaks with its soul, with that spiritual voice which is only heard by the spirit: "Man, my beloved, from within my prison of glass locked with cork, I yearn to sing you a song full of brotherhood, a song full of joy and light and expectation. I am not ungrateful; I know I owe this life to you. I know it has cost you labor with the sun beating down on your shoulders. You have given me life, and I shall recompense you . . . generously."

CHARLES BAUDELAIRE

I proffer earth's product, not
    mine
Taste, try, and approve man's
    invention of wine!
Illuminates gloom without
    sunny connivance,
Quaff wine,—how the spirits
    rise nimble and eager . . .
The juice, I uphold,
Turns fear into hope and makes
    cowardice bold,—
Touching all that is leadlike in
    life turns it to gold!

ROBERT BROWNING

Toward evening, about supper-
time, when the serious studies
of the day are over, is the time
to take wine.

CLEMENT OF ALEXANDRIA

Great wine inspires, impresses,
invigorates, and, perhaps most
significantly of all, intrigues.

JANCIS ROBINSON

Wine rejoices in the heart of
man, and joy is the mother of
every virtue. When thou hast
drunk wine, thou art ever
double what thou wouldst
otherwise be—twice as full of
ingenuity, twice as enterprising,
twice as energetic.

JOHANN WOLFGANG VON
GOETHE

Wine gives a pleasure unre-
    strain'd
Dispels the frantic spleen;
tho' wishes cannot be attain'd
looks are still joyful seen.

SIR CHARLES SEDLEY

The rapture of drinking
And wine's dizzy joy
No man who is sober deserves.

LI PO

Drinking with purpled lip the
nectar of the gods.

HORACE

Wine makes daily living easier,
less hurried, with fewer tensions
and more tolerance.

BENJAMIN FRANKLIN

The gods made wine the best thing for mortal man to scatter cares.

STASINUS OF CYPRUS

When I take wine, my cares go to rest.

ANACREON

There are no sorrows wine
    cannot allay,
There are no sins wine cannot
    wash away,
There are no riddles wine
    knows not to read,
There are no debts wine is too
    poor to pay.

RICHARD LE GALLIENNE

How long, how long, in infinite
    Pursuit
Of This and That endeavor and
    dispute?
Better be merry with the fruitful
    Grape
Than sadden after none, or
    bitter, Fruit.

OMAR KHAYYÁM

Wine drunk in season and temperately is rejoicing of heart and gladness of soul.

ECCLESIASTICUS

Wine . . . cheereth God and man.

JUDGES 9:13

Wine, like the rising sun, pos-
    session gains,
And drives the mist of dullness
    from the brains;
The gloomy vapor from the
    spirit flies,
And views of gaiety and glad-
    ness rise.

GEORGE CRABBE

Wine the consoler, the friend, the joyful companion for those who receive it in all gratitude and humility.

ANDRE L. SIMON

The best kind of wine is that which is most pleasant to him who drinks it.

PLINY THE ELDER

Wine was created from the beginning to make men joyful, and not to make them drunk.

ECCLESIASTICUS

Wine is the suitably fermented juice of the grape. Wine is the living blood of the grape. Wine is the most wholesome and beneficial beverage, one that is beyond compare as regards the antiquity, the ubiquity and the catholicity of its appeal.

ANDRE L. SIMON

All I want out of wines is to enjoy them.

ERNEST HEMINGWAY

He that drinks is immortal
For wine still supplies
What age wears away;
How can he be dust
That moistens his clay?

HENRY PURCELL

The only friends who are free from care are the goblet of wine and a book of odes.

HAFIZ

Where once my wit, perchance,
    hath shone,
In aid of others let me shine;
And when, alas! our brains are
    gone
What nobler substitute than
    wine.

GEORGE GORDON, LORD BYRON

This festive day calls for wine, for love-making and song— what fitter tribute to all-powerful gods.

OVID

Baths, wine, and Venus bring
    decay to our bodies,
But baths, wine, and Venus
    make life worth living.

LATIN EPITAPH

Wine remains a simple thing, a marriage of pleasure.

ANDRE TCHELISTCHEFF

There is no gladness without wine.

BABYLONIAN TALMUD

Good wine is nothing to rave about, but it is something to be thankful for. Fine wine, on the other hand, is a blessing.

JAMES NORWOOD PRATT

Food that is partnered with the right wine tastes better, we enjoy it more, it is digested better, and it does us good. No meal is ever dull when there is wine to drink and talk about.

ANDRE L. SIMON

A meal without wine is like making love by yourself.

JUSTIN MEYER

Wine enhances every meal . . . but to the French, wine enhances life itself.

ANDRE L. SIMON

In Europe then we thought of wine as something as healthy and normal as food and also as a great giver of happiness and well being and delight. Drinking wine was not a snobbism nor a sign of sophistication nor a cult; it was as natural as eating and to me as necessary.

ERNEST HEMINGWAY

Pshaw, ye fools that talk of
    pleasure,
 Sitting by your goblets bright!
He must be a sage can measure
 Wine's ineffable delight!

FRIEDRICH MARTIN VON
BODENSTEDT

He is not drunk who, from the
    floor,
Can rise again and drink some
    more;
But he is drunk who prostrate
    lies,
And cannot drink or cannot
    rise.

ANONYMOUS

SILENUS: But how much gold
    will you engage to give?
ULYSSES: I bring no gold, but
    Bacchic juice.
SILENUS: Oh, joy! 'Tis long since
    these dry lips were wet with
    wine.

PERCY BYSSHE SHELLEY

Good wine is a necessity of life for me.

THOMAS JEFFERSON

Wine is a magician, for it loosens the tongue and liberates good stories.

HOMER

There's no sweet in the world to
  measure
With the juice of the golden
  vine;
There's no delicate new-born
  pleasure
That can rival the rapture of
  wine.
Then let's not fear its fragrant
  perfume—
Good wine's been defamed too
  long;
For if it steals away your reason,
 It gives us love, laughter, and
  song.

For without love or wine, now
  own!
What wouldst thou be, O man!
  A stone.

GOTTHOLD LESSING

Within the bottle's depths, the wine's soul sang one night.

CHARLES BAUDELAIRE

I drink eternally. This is to me an eternity of drinking and drinking of eternity. . . . I moisten my windpipe with wine—I drink to banish all fear of dying—Drink but deep enough and you shall live forever. If the parchment on which is endorsed my bonds and bills could drink as well as I, my creditors would never need to buy wine when I settle my just dues.

FRANÇCOIS RABELAIS

Among the Egyptians of ancient times, any kind of gathering was conducted with moderation. . . . They dined while seated using the simplest and most healthful food and only as much wine as would be sufficient to promote good cheer.

ATHANASIUS

Wine—bring wine—
Flushing high with its growth
  divine,
In the crystal depth of my soul
  to shine;
Whose glow was caught
From the warmth which Fancy's
  summer brought

From the vintage fields in the
    Land of Thought.

BAYARD TAYLOR

Mingles with the friendly bowl,
The feast of reason and the flow
of soul.

ALEXANDER POPE

Fill the bowl with flowing wine,
And while your lips are wet
Press their fragrance into mine
    And forget:
Every kiss we take and give
Leaves us less of life to live.

ANONYMOUS

How sweet, as through the
    world we pass,
To find good folk who love their
    glass!
Ah! 'tis a blessing, I declare.
Surrounded by such men as
    these,
In life's warm inn I take my
    ease,
And pass without a single care
My time; and stay
An hour, a day,

Four days, a week, a month, a
    year,
And think me blest for such
    good cheer.

ANTHELME BRILLAT-SAVARIN

When the hour of mine adven-
    ture's near,
Just and benignant let my youth
    appear
Bearing a Chalice, open, golden,
    wide,
With benediction graven on its
    side.
So touch my dying lip: so bridge
    that deep:
So pledge my making from the
    gift of sleep,
And, sacramental, raise me the
    Divine:
Strong brother in God and last
    companion, Wine!

HILAIRE BELLOC

If the nymph have no compas-
    sion,
Vain it is to sigh or groan;
Love was but put in for fashion,
Wine will do the work alone.

ANONYMOUS

Wine and Creativity

*On turnpikes of wonder, wine leades
the mind forth.*

HAFIZ

The discovery of wine is of greater moment than the discovery of a constellation. The universe is too full of stars.

ANTHELME BRILLAT-SAVARIN

Quickly bring me a beaker of wine
So that I may wet my brain
And say something clever.

ARISTOPHANES

Wine, awakens and refreshes the lurking passions of the mind.

ALEXANDER POPE

Itemizing the good things in life: Money, wine and fame. Explanation: nothing could be more natural. With the money I could choose and buy the wines. The wine awakens my genius and my genius wins me fame.

CHRISTOPH GLUCK

Wine to the poet is a winged steed:
Those who drink water gain but little speed.

NICAENETUS

Great wine is a work of art. It produces a harmony of pleasing sensations which appeal directly to the aesthetic sense and at the same time sharpens the wit, gladdens the heart, and stimulates all that is most generous in human nature.

H. WARNER ALLEN

Inspiration in essence,
I am wisdom and wit to the wise,
His visible muse to the poet,
The soul of desire to the lover,
The genius of laughter to all.

ERNEST HENLEY

Let us drink to have wit, not to destroy it.

PANARD

Aristotle, the master of arts,
Had been but a dunce without wine,
And what we ascribe to his parts,
Is but due to the juice of the vine.

ANONYMOUS

And, say you so, you water-fountain-twaddler?
And dare you rail at wine's inventiveness?

For good Falernian wine.
No poet yet could praise the
     rose
In verse that so serenely flows
Unless he dipped his Roman
     nose
In good Falernian wine.

THEODORE MAYNARD

Do you remember any great
poet that ever illustrated the
higher fields of humanity that
did not dignify the use of wine
from Homer on down?

JAMES A. MCDOUGALL

I tell you nothing has such go as
     wine.
Why, look you now; 'tis when
     men drink they thrive.
Grow wealthy, speed their busi-
     ness, win their suits,
Make themselves happy, benefit
     their friends.

ARISTOPHANES

Wine is the whetstone to wit.

JONI G. MCNUTT

When Horace wrote his noble
     verse,
His brilliant, glowing line,
He must have gone to bed the
     worse

When wild with much thoughts,
'tis to wine I fly, to sober me.

HERMAN MELVILLE

What can wine perform? It
  brings to light
The secret soul, it bids the
  coward fight:
Gives being to our hopes, and
  from our hearts
Drives the dull sorrow, and
  inspires new arts.

HORACE

Wine whets the wit, improves its
native force, and gives a pleasant
flavour to discourse.

JOHN POMFRET

If with water you fill up your
  glasses,
You'll never write anything wise;
For wine is the horse of Parnassus,

Which hurries a bard to the
  skies.

THOMAS MOORE

In certain studies, there is no
harm in doing one's thinking
and writing while slightly
drunk, and then revising one's
work in cold blood. The stim-
ulus of wine is favorable to the
play of invention, and to fluency
of expression.

G. C. LICHTENBERG

Wine, n. Fermented, grape juice
known to the Women's Chris-
tian Union as 'liquor,' some

Drink oftener, though with
    modesty
And prove yourself the wiser
Than this old pinching,
    scrimping dame
Full of remorse we find her
The devil carries her to Hell
Her wine stays behind her.

ANONYMOUS

Let those who drink not, but
    austerely dine,
Dry up in law; the Muses smell
    of wine.

HORACE

times as 'rum.' Wine, madam, is
God's next best gift to man.

AMBROSE BIERCE

If I write a verse, or two,
'Tis with very much ado;
In regard I want that Wine,
Which sho'd conjure up a line.

ROBERT HERRICK

And when we pour libations
to the gods, we pour the god of
    wine himself
that through his intercession
    man may win
the favor of heaven.

EURIPIDES

I, Bacchus, tell thee, worthy
    friend
Be with good wine no miser

For of all labours, none tran-
    scend
The works that on the brain
    depend;
Nor could we finish great
    designs
Without the power of generous
    wines.

ANONYMOUS

Tasting

*To take wine into our mouths is to savor a droplet of
the river of human history.*

CLIFTON FADIMAN

Get a wineglass that exposes the wine to plenty of air. The more air you can expose wine to, the better you can taste it. And be sure you can get your nose in the glass. That's important because in wine-tasting, the nose does seventy-five percent of the work. A glass with a three-inch rim is best for most wines. But if you have a larger than average nose, you'll need a larger-than-average glass.

INGLENOOK WINERY

       The secret of getting the maximum pleasure out of wine is to remember that we smell tastes; it is our noses and the nerves high in the brain behind the nasal cavity that distinguish nuances of flavours—not our tongues, lips or palates. The mouth detects what is sweet, sour, salt, bitter, burning, smooth, oily, astringent. But the colour and character of a flavour lies in its volatile compounds which need the nose to apprehend them. Thus, the procedure for tasting wine pivots around the moment of inhalation: the crucial first sniff.

HUGH JOHNSON

You can talk about wine as if it were a bunch of flowers (fragrant, heavily perfumed); a packet of razor blades (steely); a navy (robust, powerful); a troupe of acrobats (elegant and

I was convinced forty years ago—and the conviction remains to this day—that in wine tasting and wine-talk there is an enormous amount of humbug.

THOMAS GEORGE SHAW

well balanced); a successful industrialist (distinguished and rich); a virgin in a bordello (immature and giving promise of pleasure to come); Brighton Beach (clean and pebbly); even a potato (earthy) or a Christmas pudding (plump, sweet and round).

DEREK COOPER

The important thing with the 1874 Lafite is to taste the wine in its historical context. In 1874 the Impressionists were painting, Brahms was composing, and Paris was just over the Commune.

MICHAEL BROADBENT

Deep colour and big shaggy nose. Rather a jumbly, untidy sort of wine, with fruitiness shooting off one way, firmness another, and body pushing about underneath. It will be as comfortable and as comforting as the 1961 Nuits St. Georges once it has pulled its ends in and settled down.

GERALD ASHER

The art of tasting wine is the performance of a sacred rite, which deserves to be carried out with the most grave and serious attention.

FRENCH NATIONAL
COMMITTEE FOR WINE
PUBLICITY

At the first sip, a good drinker should recognize the vineyard, at the second, the quality, and at the third, the year.

ALEXANDER DUMAS

The aristocrat of the table, the nature's gentleman of the cellar, the true *amateur*, the deeply knowledgeable, is rarely, if ever, a snob.

MICHAEL BROADBENT

A truly great wine with brilliant color, subtle bouquet, perfect balance and lingering taste is a sensuous experience and a work of art.

KENNETH MACDONALD AND
TOM THROCKMORTON

An old wine bibber, having been smashed in a railway collision, some wine was poured on his lips to revive him. "Pauillac, 1873," he murmured, and died.

AMBROSE BIERCE

Wine lives and dies; it has not only its hot youth, strong maturity and weary dotage, but also its seasonal changes, its mysterious, almost mystical, link with its parent vine, so that when the sap is running in the wood on the middle slopes of the Côte d'Or, in a thousand cellars, a thousand miles away, the wine in its bottle quickens and responds.

EVELYN WAUGH

Wine is like music—you may not know what good is, but you know what you like!

JUSTIN MEYER

Wine is, indeed, a living thing, brash in its youth, full-blossoming it its maturity, but subject, if not used in time, to senility, decay and death.

ANDRE L. SIMON

A jar of wine so priceless did not deserve to die.

MARTIAL

The flavor of wine is like delicate poetry.

LOUIS PASTEUR

Wine of California . . . inimitable fragrance and soft fire . . . and the wine is bottled poetry.

ROBERT LOUIS STEVENSON

Grudge myself a good wine?—as soon as grudge my horse corn.

WILLIAM MAKEPEACE THACKERAY

He that is penniless is rich, and even the wealthy find their hearts expanding when they are smitten by the arrows of the vine.

PINDAR

The first obligation of a great wine is to be red.

HENRI MURGER

Years ago, when I was living very briefly with a stockbrocker who had a good cellar, I asked him how I could learn about wine. "Drink it," he said.

JEANNETTE WINTERSON

There is no substitute for pulling corks.

ALEXIS LICHINE

Sometimes you have to stop and sniff the corks.

ARNA DAN ISACSSON

A sight of the label is worth fifty years' experience.

MICHAEL BROADBENT

I can name the claret if I see the cork.

OLIVER WENDELL HOLMES

I had just taken a swig of some smooth and velvety liquid that lingered in my mouth with a distant memory of wild strawberries. . . .

"Over there, in case you're looking for it. Expectoration corner!" Bertie waved me to a wooden wine-box, half filled with sawdust, into which the gents in dark suitings were directing mouthfuls of purplish liquid. I moved away from him, reluctant to admit that such wine as I had been able to win had long since disappeared down the little red lane.

JOHN MORTIMER

Bad wine does me no harm, because it never gets past my nose.

GEORGE SANDEMAN

There is not the hundredth part of the wine consumed in this kingdom that there ought to be. Our foggy climate wants help.

JANE AUSTEN

The wine in the bottle does not quench thirst.

GEORGE HERBERT

That little sentence "have the chill taken off" has done more harm to good wine than it is possible to imagine.

MARCEL BOULESTIN

Wine snobbery, of course, is part showmanship, part sophistication, part knowledge and part bluff.

LEONARD BERNSTEIN

The wines that one remembers best are not necessarily the finest that one has tasted, and the highest quality may fail to delight so much as some far more humble beverage drunk in more favourable surroundings.

H. WARNER ALLEN

The alcohol in wine is as the canvas upon which an artist paints a picture. . . . It is not the small percentage of alcohol that appeals to you, but the brilliant ruby of the wine's colour, the attractive perfume of its bouquet and the delicious savour of its farewell, the lingering taste which it leaves behind as it descends smoothly down your grateful throat.

ANDRE L. SIMON

For a gourmet, wine is not a drink but a condiment, provided that your host has chosen it correctly.

EDOUARD DE POMAINE

You yourself, my lord Prior, like to drink the best. So does any honest man; never does a man of worth dislike good wine: it is a monastical apothegm.

FRANÇOIS RABELAIS

The earlier stages of the dinner had worn off. The wine lists had been consulted, with some of the blank embarrassment of a schoolboy suddenly called on to locate a Minor Prophet in the tangled hinterland of the Old Testament, by others with the severe scrutiny which suggests that they have visited most of the higher-priced wines in their own homes and probed their family weaknesses.

SAKI

As long as the wine is in the mouth, one receives a pleasant but indistinct impression; it is only when one has finished swallowing it that one can really taste, appreciate and identify its particular bouquet; and a short while must elapse before the gourmand can say: 'It's good, or passable, or bad. Bless my soul! It's Chambertin! Good grief! It's Suresnes!' True connoisseurs *sip* their wine; for as they pause after each mouthful, they obtain the sum total of pleasure they would have experienced had they emptied the glass at a single draught.

ANTHELME BRILLAT-SAVARIN

Moselle is like the girl of four-
teen to eighteen: light, quick on
the tongue, with an exquisite,
evanescent perfume, but little
body. It may be used constantly
and in quantities, but must be
taken young.

FRANK HARRIS

Bouquet is the soul of the wine,
while an agreeable aroma
unfailingly imparts a delicious
sensation.

FIONA EUNICE WAIT

It is true that taste can be edu-
cated. It is also true that taste
can be perverted. . . . If any man
gives you a wine you can't bear,
don't say it is beastly. . . . but
don't say you like it. You are
endangering your soul and the
use of wine as well. Seek out
some other wine good to your
taste.

HILAIRE BELLOC

Winetasting, in the classic
phrase, is a diverting pastime
for young and old, for ladies as
well as men. It is not so intellectual as chamber-music, it is not

so light-hearted as striptease; no
one will burst into "Ach, du
lieber Augustin" as he waves his
tiny libation of some promising
new vintage around his head,
nor will anyone entangle you
with problems that need an
intimate understanding of Ein-
stein and a slide-rule to answer.
It is, in fact, the ideal pursuit
with which to while away those
hours between eleven in the
morning and four in the after-
noon.

B. A. YOUNG

Quality in wines is much easier
to recognize than to define.

MAYNARD A. AMERINE

As in lovemaking, reading is a
damn poor substitute for experience in the gentle art of [wine]
tasting. It is one of those things
you find out by yourself.

JAMES NORWOOD PRATT

I know of no other liquid that,
placed in the mouth, forces one
to think.

CLIFTON FADIMAN

To appreciate truly a wine that
    is "great",
Don't drink it too hastily, thirst
    to abate.
First, hold up the glass, the fine
    color to see.
Next, rotate it gently, the bou-
    quet to free.
Then third, sip it slowly to savor
    its strength.
Last, put the glass down, discuss
    it at length.

ANONYMOUS

After melon, wine is a felon.

ITALIAN PROVERB

Effects of Wine

Wine rejoices the heart of man, and joy is the mother of all virtue.
JOHANN WOLFGANG VON GOETHE

The smaller the drink, the
clearer the head.

WILLIAM PENN

Wine, the cheerer of the heart
And lively refresher of the coun-
tenance.

THOMAS MIDDLETON AND
WILLIAM ROWLEY

Give me a bowl of wine
In this I bury all unkindness.

WILLIAM SHAKESPEARE

Wine is a mocker, strong drink
is raging: and whosoever is
deceived thereby is not wise.

PROV. 20:1

Wine makes a man better
pleased with himself. . . . But the
danger is that while a man
grows better pleased with himself, he may be growing less
pleasing to others.

SAMUEL JOHNSON

The secret of drunkenness is
that it insulates us in thought,
whilst it unites us in feeling.

RALPH WALDO EMERSON

It is better to hide ignorance,
but it is hard to do this when
relaxed over wine.

HERACLITUS

Wine turns a man inside out-
wards.

THOMAS FULLER

When wine goes in, stranger
things come out.

JOHANN VON SCHILLER

I am falser than the vows made
in wine.

WILLIAM SHAKESPEARE

The wine urges men on, the
bewitching wine, which sets
even a wise man to singing and
to laughing gently and rouses
him up to dance and brings
forth words which were better
unspoken.

HOMER

Pure wine indeed! Is this a
tippling matter?
How can one get, when drunk, a
happy thought?

NICIAS

One must always be drunk. Everything is there: It is the essential issue. To avoid that horrible burden of Time grabbing your shoulders and crushing you to the earth, you must get drunk without restraint. But on what? On wine, poetry or virtue, whatever you fancy. But get drunk.

CHARLES BAUDELAIRE

There's no law possible without wine. Law is an occupation which dries the blood.

GEORGE MEREDITH

A vine bears three grapes, the first of pleasure, the second of intoxication, and the third of repentance.

ANACHARSIS

No nation is drunken where wine is cheap; and none sober where the dearness of wine substitutes ardent spirits as the common beverage. It is, in truth, the only antidote to the bane of whiskey.

THOMAS JEFFERSON

The dipsomaniac and the abstainer both make the same mistake: they both regard wine as a drug and not as a drink.

G. K. CHESTERTON

In introducing this grape to public notice, I have done my country a greater service than I should have done had I paid the national debt.

JOHN ADLUM

Polished brass is the mirror of the body and wine of the heart.

AESCHYLUS

'Tween woman and wine, a
    man's lot is to smart
For wine makes his head ache,
    and woman his heart.

ANONYMOUS

One of the disadvantages of wine is that it makes a man mistake words for thoughts.

SAMUEL JOHNSON

When the head is under the influence of wine, many a thing swims out of the heart.

YUGOSLAV PROVERB

Counsels in wine seldom prosper.

ENGLISH PROVERB

Take especial care that thou delight not in wine; for there never was any man that came to honour or preferment that loved it; for it transformeth a man into a beast, decayeth health, poisoneth the breath, destroyeth natural heat, deformeth the face, rotteth the teeth, and maketh a man contemptible.

SIR WALTER RALEIGH

The intemperate drinking of wine causes a chilliness of the blood, a dissolution of the nerves, a dissipation of the generative seed, a numbness of the senses, a distortion of movement, which are all impediments to the act of generation. This is why you see Bacchus, king of drunkards, depicted beardless and in woman's dress, as an effeminate and ball-less eunuch.

FRANCOIS RABELAIS

Boys should abstain from all use of wine until their eighteenth year, for it is wrong to add fire to fire.

PLATO

When a man eats the fruit of the vine, he is as gentle as a lamb; when he drinks wine, he believes himself a lion; if, by chance, he drinks too much, he grimaces like a monkey; and when he is often drunk, he is nothing more than a vile pig.

THE TALMUD

Then when the wild men knew
The scent of honeyed wine that
        tames men's souls,
Straight from the board they
        thrust the milk-bowls
With hurrying hands, and of
        their own will flew
To the horns of silver wrought
And drank and were distraught.

PINDAR

Wine makes the eye quick to see, turns all things fairer and brings back the blessings of fair youth.

MAECENAS

Tarry till I bring thee
honey-sweet wine, that thou
mayest pour libation to Zeus
and all the immortals first, and
then shalt thou thyself also be
refreshed if thou wilt drink.

HOMER

So Noah, when he anchor'd safe
    on
The mountain's top, his lofty
    haven,
And all the passengers he bore
Were on the new world set
    ashore,
He made it next his chief design
To plant and propagate a vine,
Which since has overwhelm'd
    and drown'd
Far greater numbers, on dry
    ground,
Of wretched mankind, one by
    one,
Than all the flood before had
    done.

SAMUEL BUTLER

Drink not the third glass, which
    thou canst not tame,
When once it is within thee.

GEORGE HERBERT

Count not the cups; not therein
    lies excess
In wine, but in the nature of the
    drinker.

MENANDER

Too much and too little wine.
Give him none, he cannot find
truth; give him too much, the
same.

BLAISE PASCAL

Bring me no honey heartened
wine, my lady mother, lest thou
cripple me of my courage and I
be forgetful of my might.

HOMER

Where wine is lacking, drugs are
necessary.

THE TALMUD

Give strong drink unto him that
is ready to perish and wine unto
those that be of heavy hearts.
Let him drink, and forget his
poverty and remember his
misery no more.

PROV. 31:6-7

Then trust me, there's nothing
   like drinking
So pleasant on this side the
   grave;
It keeps the unhappy from
   thinking,
And makes e'en the valiant
   more brave.

CHARLES DIBDIN

Who hath woe? who hath
sorrow? who hath contentions?
who hath babbling? who hath
wounds without cause? who
hath redness of eyes? They that
tarry long at the wine.

PROV. 23:29

Lazarus, you are more indebted
to wine than to your father, for
he gave you life but once, while
wine has given it back to you a
thousand times.

SPANISH SOURCE

. . . wine does not isolate but
binds men together.

CLIFTON FADIMAN

A man cannot make him laugh;
but that's no marvel; he drinks
no wine.

WILLIAM SHAKESPEARE

Wine makes old wives wenches.

JOHN CLARKE

It is to wine that humankind is
indebted for being the only
creatures that drink without
being thirsty.

PLINY THE YOUNGER

When the strength of wine has
hit, our limbs become heavy, we
lurch and trip over our legs, our
speech slurs, our minds become
sodden, our eyes glazed. Then
comes the din, hiccoughs and
fights.

LUCRETIUS

What has been said drunk has
been thought out beforehand.

FLEMISH PROVERB

Give a scholler wine, going to
his booke, or being about to
invent, it sets a new poynt on
his wit, it glazeth it, it scowres
it, it give him acumen.

THOMAS NASHE

Wine at a feast gives less joy
than the mourning of an enemy.

MARQUISE DE SÉVIGNÉ

Here, waiter, more wine, let me
sit while I'm able
Till all my companions sink
    under the table.

OLIVER GOLDSMITH

The man that isn't too jolly after
    drinking
Is just a driveling idiot, to my
    thinking.

EURIPIDES

Within this goblet, rich and
    deep,
I cradle all my woes to sleep.

TOM MOORE

A bottle of good wine, like a
good act, shines ever in retrospect.

ROBERT LOUIS STEVENSON

One can learn about wine and
pursue the education of one's
palate with great enjoyment all
of a lifetime . . . even though the
kidneys may weaken, the big toe
become painful, the finger joints
stiffen, until finally, just when
you love it the most, you are
forbidden wine entirely. . . . I
would rather have a palate that
will give me the pleasure of

enjoying completely a Chateau
Margaux or a Haut Brion, even
though excesses indulged in the
acquiring of it have brought a
liver that will not allow me to
drink Richebourg, Corton, or
Chambertin, than to have the
corrugated iron internals of my
boyhood when all red wines
were bitter, except Port, and
drinking was the process of
getting down enough of anything to make you feel reckless.

ERNEST HEMINGWAY

Fill ev'ry glass, for wine inspires
    us,
And fires us
With courage, love, and joy.
Women and wine should life
    employ.
Is there aught else on earth
    desirous?

JOHN GAY

The six cup makes me wise with
wine,
A thousand riddles clear as
crystal shine;
And much I wonder what it can
have been
That used to puzzle this poor
head of mine.
Yet with the morn the
wine-deserted brain
Sees all its riddles trooping back
again:—
Say, am I sober when I see
naught clear?
And am I drunk when I see all
things plain?

RICHARD LE GALLIENNE

And all through the term of his
life, man has much to learn,
much to bear and suffer—trials,
doubts, injustice, failures—but
he also has much help—faith,
friendship, success and the tonic
that is wine. Wine is to the
parched mind of man what
water is to the sun-drenched
plain. It releases the brakes of
his self-consciousness and
softens the hard-baked crust of
dust so that the seeds below
may send forth sweet flowers.

ANDRE L. SIMON

When wine I quaff, before my
eyes
Dreams of poetic glory rise;
And, freshen'd by the goblet's
dews,
My soul invokes the heavenly
Muse.
When wine I drink, all sorrow's
o'er;
I think of doubts and fears no
more;
But scatter to the railing wind
Each gloomy phantom of the
mind.
When I drink wine, the ethereal
boy,
Bacchus himself, partakes my
joy;
And while we dance through
vernal bowers,
Whose ev'ry breath comes fresh
from flowers,
In wine he makes my senses
swim,
Till the gale breathes nought but
him!

ANACREON

What cannot wine perform? It
brings to light
The secret soul; it bids the
coward fight:
Gives being to our hopes, and
from our hearts

Drives the dull sorrow, and
    inspires new arts.

ANONYMOUS

What tongue hangs fire when
    quickened by the bowl?
What wretch so poor but wine
    expands his soul?

HORACE

Brisk methinks I am, and fine,
When I drinke my carping wine:
Then to love I do encline;
When I drinke my wanton wine:
And I wish all maidens mine,
When I drinke my sprightly
    wine:
Well I sup, and well I dine,
When I drinke my frolick wine:
But I languish, lowre, and Pine,
When I want my fragrant wine.

ROBERT HERRICK

Give me a bowl of wine.
I have not that alacrity of spirit
Nor cheer of mind that I was
    wont to have.

WILLIAM SHAKESPEARE

Smooth out with wine the
worries of a wrinkled brow.

HORACE

Wine is the milk of the old, the
balm of adults and the vehicle
of the gourmand.

A. B. L. GRIMOND DE LA
REYNIERE

Wine makes love forget its care,
And mirth exalts a feast.

THOMAS PARNELL

Wine can of their wits the wise
    beguile,
Make the sage frolic, and the
    serious smile.

ALEXANDER POPE

Bacchus drowns within the bowl
Troubles that corrode the soul.

HORACE

Wine is like life to men, if you
drink it in moderation. What is
life to a man who is without
wine? It has been created to
make men glad.

ECCLESIASTICUS

[Wine is] the philosopher which
drives away care, and makes us
forget whatever is disagreeable.

OLIVER GOLDSMITH

Wine timely given aids untimely opportunities.

PROPERTIUS

Wine is the glass of the mind.

ERASMUS

Wine brings to light the hidden secrets of the soul.

HORACE

With mirth and laughter, let old
    wrinkles come,
And let my liver, rather heat
    with wine,
Than my heart cool with morti-
    fying gloom.

WILLIAM SHAKESPEARE

Wine opens the heart.
Opens it! It thaws it right out.

HERMAN MELVILLE

Wine invents nothing; it only tattles.

J. C. F. VON SCHILLER

Wine leads to folly. It makes even the wisest laugh too much. It makes him dance. It makes him say what should have been left unsaid.

HOMER

Three glasses of wine can set everything to rights.

CHINESE PROVERB

A friend and a bottle is all my
    design;
He has no room for treason
    that's top-full of wine.

JOHN OLDHAM

Wine gives strength to weary men.

HOMER

Wine is like rain: when it falls
    on the mire it makes it the
    fouler,
But when it strikes the good
    soil, wakes it to beauty and
    blooms.

JOHN HAY

Wine can clear the vapors of
    despair
And make us light as air.

JOHN GAY

When men drink wine, they are rich, they are busy, they push lawsuits, they are happy, they help their friends.

ARISTOPHANES

Wine is good,
Love is good,
And all is good if understood;
The sin is not in doing,
But in overdoing.
How much of mine has gone
    that way!
Alas! how much more that may!

ANONYMOUS

Good wine makes good blood,
Good blood causeth good
    humours,
Good humours cause good
    thoughts,
Good thoughts bring forth good
    works,
Good works carry a man to
    heaven.
Ergo,
Good wine carrieth a man to
    heaven.

JOHN MINSHEU

They [the Persians] are accustomed to deliberate on matters of the highest moment when warm with wine; but whatever they . . . may determine is again proposed to them on the morrow, in their cooler moments. If at this time also it meet their approbation, it is executed; otherwise it is rejected. Whatever also they discuss when sober, is always a second time examined after they have been drinking.

HERODOTUS

Three cups of wine a prudent
    man may take:
The first of them for constitu-
    tion sake;
The second to the girl he loves
    the best;
The third and last, to lull him to
    his rest—
Then home to bed. But if a
    fourth he pours,
That is the cup of folly, and not
    ours.
Loud noisy talking on the fifth
    attends;
The sixth breeds feuds and
    falling out of friends;
Seven beget blows, and faces
    stained with gore;
Eight, and the watch patrol
    breaks ope' the door;
Mad with the ninth, another
    cup goes round,
And the swilled sot drops sense-
    less on the ground.

ATHANASIUS

He turn'd a fruit to
    an enchantment
Which cheers the sad,
    revives the old, inspires
The young, makes
    weariness forget his toil,
And fear her danger,
    opens a new world
When this, the present palls.

GEORGE GORDON, LORD
BYRON

Wine hath drowned more men
than the sea.

THOMAS FULLER

Wine is a turncoat—first a
friend, then an enemy.

GEORGE HERBERT

Wine heightens indifference into
love, love into jealousy, and
jealousy into madness. It often
turns the good-natured man
into an idiot, and the choleric
man into an assassin. It gives
bitterness to resentment, makes
vanity unsupportable, and
displays every little spot of the
soul in its utmost deformity.

JOSEPH ADDISON

'Tis pity wine should be so
    deleterious,
For tea and coffee leave us much
    more serious.

GEORGE GORDON, LORD
BYRON

Wine is a discoverer of secrets.

CHINESE PROVERB

Wine is a peep-hole on a man.

ALCAEUS

Come, come, good wine is a
good familiar creature, if it be
well used; exclaim no more
against it.

WILLIAM SHAKESPEARE

[Wine] helps us to penetrate the
veil; it gives us glimpses of the
Magi of creation where they sit
weaving their spells and sowing
their seeds of incantation to the
flowing mind.

DON MARQUIS

Making of Wine

Wine was not invented. It was born. Man has done no more than learn to educate.

J. M. SCOTT

Wine, the most delightful of drinks, whether we owe it to Noah, who planted the vine, or to Bacchus, who pressed the juice from the grape, goes back to the childhood of the world.

ANTHELME BRILLAT-SAVARIN

Season of mists
    and mellow fruitfulness,
Close-bosom friend
    of the maturing sun:
Conspiring with him
    how to load and bless
With fruit the vines that
    round the thatch-eves run.

JOHN KEATS

Ash stakes for the forked
    uprights,
Upon whose strength your vines
    can mount
And be trained to clamber
Up the high-storied elm
    trees. . . .

VIRGIL

Wine is a living thing, not a mere chemical composition; like any living organism, it is young, grows old, and eventually decays and dies, the cycle of its life depending on that of the fermentation microbes which bestow on it its nature and excellence.

H. WARNER ALLEN

A bunch of grapes is beautiful, static and innocent. It is merely fruit. But when it is crushed, it becomes an animal, for the crushed grapes become wine and wine has an animal life. Wine suffers a heaving birth. It has a rough, groping childhood. It develops into adolescence. Then, if it does not sicken, it matures; and in this it is almost human since it does not mature according to a fixed rule but according to the law of its particular and individual personality.

WILLIAM YOUNGER

The Grape that can with Logic
    absolute
The Two-and-Seventy jarring
    Sects confute:
The sovereign Alchemist that in
    a trice
Life's leaden metal into Gold
    transmute.

OMAR KHAYYÁM

Back of this wine is the vintner,
And back through the years his
    skill,
And back of it all are the vines
    in the sun
And the rain and the Master's
    Will.

VINTNER'S ODE

Beer is made by men, wine by
God!

MARTIN LUTHER

Good days are to be gathered
like sunshine in grapes, to be
trodden and bottled into wine
and kept for age to sip at ease
beside his fire. If the traveller
has vintaged well, he need
trouble to wander no longer; the
ruby moments glow in his glass
at will.

FREYA STARK

Was it not the skillful hand of
Osiris that indicated how to join
the young vine to the pole, how
to lop the green leaves with the
grim hook of the pruner? For
him the ripe grapes, crushed by
trampling feet, first yielded up
their agreeable flavour. Their
juice taught men to attune the
voice to mirth and sorrow, and
told unaccustomed limbs to
move in gracious harmony.
When the heart of the peasant is
crushed with arduous labour, it
is Bacchus who draws it back to
joyfulness, loosens it from the
bands of sorrow. To mortals
wrapt in distress, the Wine-god
brings relief, even though the
hated gyves* encompass their
legs.

ALBIUS TIBULLUS

You get the best vintage from
well-cared-for grapes.

OVID

Making good wine is a skill, fine
wine, an art.

ROBERT MONDAVI

*leg irons

I create a prodigious flurry in the worker's stomach and from there by invisible staircases I climb to his brain where I perform my supreme dance. Do you hear stirring and re-echoing mighty choruses of ancient times in me, songs of love and glory? I am the soul of your homeland, part troubadour and part soldier. The hope of Sundays am I. Work makes for prosperous weekdays, wine for happy Sundays. With your sleeves rolled up and your elbows on the family table, you will glory in me proudly and you will be truly content.

CHARLES BAUDELAIRE

However old it may be, the great vintage dates from far long before the starting points of its brief existence, the shaping forces were in play; it draws its excellence from origins deep buried in the earth from which it came. Before it could begin to be born it was necessary that the earth where it was engendered should become a thing ancient in use, and that its cradle should be a tomb full of ashes of the years and dust of the centuries.

M. GASTON RONPULE,
QUOTED BY ALEC WAUGH

I must look over the vines again
   where my childhood days
   were spent,
See the young roots and the old
   roots which have now
   become gnarled and bent;
And all I ask is a jug of wine
   from the grapes my sons
   have tended,
And to know the vineyard will
   yet be tilled when the long
   day's ended.

ROBIN BLACKBURNE

And that you may the less
   marvel at my words,
Look at the sun's heat that
   becomes the wine
When combined with the juice
   that flows from the vine.

DANTE

Old timers believe the quality of a man's wine depends on his own quality and character, a little bit of himself going into every bottle. To gain lasting fame, he has to be a poet, a philosopher and an honorable man, as well as a master craftsman.

PETER MONDAVI

God made only water, but man made wine.

VICTOR HUGO

Wine was born, not invented. . . . Like an old friend, it continues to surprise us in new and unexpected ways.

SALVATORE P. LUCIA, M.D.

Cellars are not catacombs. They are, if rightly constructed, cloisters where the bottle meditates on joys to bestow, not on dust misused.

GEORGE MEREDITH

A stubborn thing, your lord-
　　ships, is the soil
And he must it hoe
Water it with salty drops
That from his face do flow,
Raising your glasses, think
Of this hard toil,
And find it meet,
The People's health to drink.

ANONYMOUS

Wine and Friendship

From wine what sudden friendship springs!

JOHN GAY

Wine seems to have the power of attracting friendship, warming and fusing hearts together.

ATHANASIUS

One cannot imagine the wine drinker in solitude. . . . The real lover of wine can only enjoy it along with friends, sharing with them the art of conversation and the art of drinking. Wine is indeed essentially a sign of civilization, a factor of sociability, friendship.

JEAN DRAPEAU

I love everything that's old: old friends, old times, old manners, old books, old wines.

OLIVER GOLDSMITH

"I am beauty and love;
I am friendship, the comforter;
I am that which forgives and
    forgets."
    The Spirit of Wine
    Sang in my heart, and I
        triumphed

In the savour and scent of
    his music,
    His magnetic and mas-
        tering song.

W. E. HENLEY

A book of verses and a cup of
    pure wine,
Are truly your most intimate
    friends.
Watch your road for it has
    curves and bends;
Enjoy wine for only once is life
    thine.

HAFIZ

Over a bottle of wine, many a friend is found.

YIDDISH PROVERB

The drinking of wine seems to have a moral edge over many pleasures and hobbies in that it promotes love of one's neighbor. As a general thing, it is not a lone occupation. A bottle of wine begs to be shared; I have never met a miserly wine lover.

CLIFTON FADIMAN

Selfishness is a vice unknown to the wine-lover.

H. WARNER ALLEN

Old wine and an old friend are good provisions.

GEORGE HERBERT

Wine is the only natural beverage that feeds not only the body, but the soul and spirit of man; stimulates the mind and creates a more gracious and happy way of life.

ROBERT MONDAVI

He who has wealth and wine will always have friends.

CHINESE PROVERB

What though youth gave love and roses, age still leaves us friends and wine.

THOMAS MOORE

Better is old wine than new, and old friends likewise.

CHARLES KINGSLEY

When you ask one friend to
    dine,
Give him your best wine!
When you ask two,
The second best will do!

HENRY WADSWORTH
LONGFELLOW

Good company, good wine, good welcome, make good people.

WILLIAM SHAKESPEARE

With each glass of this wine, I double the number of friends I have in this room.

ANONYMOUS

Old friends know what I like:
They bring wine whenever they
    come by.
We spread out and sit under the
    pines;
After several rounds, we're
    drunk again.
Old men chatting away—all at
    once;
Passing the jug around—out of
    turn.
Unaware that there is a "self,"
How do we learn to value
    "things"?
We are lost in these deep
    thoughts;
In wine, there is a heady taste.

T'AO CHI'EN

Friends and wine should be old.

SPANISH PROVERB

While wine and friendship
　　crown the board,
We'll sing the joys that both
　　afford;
And he that won't with us
　　comply,
Down among the dead men let
　　him lie.

JOHN DYER

Good friends, go in and taste
some wine with me; and we like
friends will straightway go
together.

WILLIAM SHAKESPEARE

With a dear friend, a thousand
cups of wine are too few.

CHINESE PROVERB

Fan the sinking flame of hilarity
with the wing of friendship; and
pass the rosy.

CHARLES DICKENS

Wine-lovers are unselfish folk.
Few, if any of them, care to
drink their choicest wine, when
they are alone. For that experience loses half its fascination if
it is not accompanied by the
conversation of good fellowship
and that discussion of the wine,
which carries its memory to the
gods by apt comparisons and
seasoned praise based on the
remembrance of other wines. I
have heard of egotists who
sought to buy up all the bottles
that remained of some rare
vintage that they might have the
satisfaction of knowing that no
other oenologist, no other con-
noisseur, could set it on his
table, but even then their selfishness was concerned not with
the greediness of drinking it
themselves, but with the more
generous vanity of offering it to
their friends.

H. WARNER ALLEN

Wine and Love

After wyn, on Venus moste I thinke.

GEOFFREY CHAUCER

God made man, frail as a
    bubble;
Man made love—love made
    trouble.
God made the vine—
Then is it a sin
That man made wine
To drown trouble in?

OLIVER HERFORD

Bring water, bring wine, boy!
Bring flowering garlands to me!
Yes, bring them, so that I may
try a bout with love.

ANACREON

What man can pretend to be a
believer in love, who is an
abjurer of wine?

RICHARD BRINSLEY
SHERIDAN

Who does not love wine,
women, and song remains a fool
his whole life long.

JOHANN VOSS

Wine it is the milk of Venus,
And the poet's horse accounted:
Ply it and you all are mounted.

BEN JONSON, OVER THE
DOOR AT THE DEVIL TAVERN

I make love to good wine and to
drinking.

ETIENNE PASQUIER

Wine gives courage and makes
men apt for passion.

OVID

Here's to Love and Laughter,
I'll be true as long as you,
But not a moment after.

ANONYMOUS

Alas, alas, in ways so dark,
'Tis only wine can strike a
spark.

ANACREON

Drink, luckless lover! Thy
    heart's fiery rape,
Bacchus, who gives oblivion,
    shall assuage;
Drink deep; and while thou
    drain'st the brimming bowl,
Drive love's dark anguish from
    thy fevered soul.

MELEAGER

Wine gives you liberty, love
takes it away.

WILLIAM WYCHERLY

In water one sees one's own face; but in wine one beholds the heart of another.

FRENCH PROVERB

It warms the blood, adds luster to the eyes,
And wine and love have ever been allies.

OVID

New loves and old wines:
Give a man these and he never repines.

FRANCIS BEEDING

There is wan thing an' on'y wan thing to be said in favor iv dhrink, an' that is that it has caused many a lady to be loved that otherwise might've died single.

FINLEY PETER DUNNE

Wine is a precarious aphrodisiac, and its fumes have blighted many a mating.

NORMAN DOUGLAS

Where there is no wine, love perishes, and everything else that is pleasant to man.

EURIPIDES

Wine and Love have ever been allies;
But carefully from all intemperance keep,
Nor drink till you see double, lisp or sleep.

OVID

Wine lets no lover unrewarded go.

ALEXANDER POPE

Without food and wine, love starves.

TERENTIUS

The best wine for my beloved, that goeth down sweetly, causing the lips of those that are asleep to speak.

SONG OF SOLOMON 7:9

Wine prepares the heart for love,
Unless you take too much.

OVID

Nothing is more useful than wine for strengthening the body and also more detrimental to our pleasures if moderation be lacking.

PLINY THE ELDER

I told you I was drained of
    happiness.
The wine was only half-way
    down our glasses.
You said to me, "Are you not
    happy now?"
Searching my heart, I had to
    own I was.
How should I not be, drinking
    wine with you?
"Whatever dies was not mixed
    equally,"
Donne said. If so, love is
    without death,
For half the happiness of
    meeting you
Is pain at knowing we must
    separate;
And therefore love can never be
    complete.
A glass untasted and an empty
    glass,
Are nothing but mere hope and
    memory.
The glass in which I drink your
    health contains
Now and always half wine, half
    emptiness.

    JAMES REEVES

What is love without the bowl?
'Tis a languor of the soul.
Crowned with ivy, Venus
    charms;

Ivy courts me to her arms.
Bacchus, give me love and wine,
Happiness is only thine!

    THOMAS CHATTERTON

All my pleasure is to sip
Wine from my beloved's lip;
I have gained the utmost bliss—
God alone be praised for this.

    HAFIZ

We swam and sunned as well as
    drank,
And found all heaven in a word;
But, dearest Thea, to be frank,
I think we had the wine to
    thank
For most of what occurred.

    ANONYMOUS

Wine and Water

Th' water hurteth, wyne maketh one sing.

JOHN FLORIO

I fear the man who drinks water
And so remembers next
   morning
What the rest of us said last
   night.

GREEK PROVERB

Wine is the drink of the gods,
milk the drink of babies, tea the
drink of women, and water the
drink of beasts.

JOHN STUART BLACKIE

Water . . . doth very greatly
deject the appetite, destroy the
natural heat, and overthrow the
strength of the stomach.

TOBIAS VENNER

Wine to a gifted bard,
Is a mount that merrily races;
From watered wits
No good has ever grown.

CRATINUS QUOTED BY
NICAENETUS

To drink wine is to be a good
Catholic. . . . To drink only
water, and to have a hatred for
wine, is pure heresy, close to
atheism.

BEROALDE DE VERVILLE

It was a very Corsican wine and you could dilute it by half with water and still receive its message.

ERNEST HEMINGWAY

Water, taken in moderation, cannot hurt anybody.

MARK TWAIN

Wine is light, held together by water.

GALILEO

A man who drinks only water has a secret to hide from his fellow-men.

CHARLES BAUDELAIRE

Here's to water, water divine
It dews the grapes that gives us
    the wine.

ANONYMOUS

And Noah he often said to his
    wife
    when he sat down to dine,
"I don't care where the water
        goes if
    it doesn't get into the wine."

G. K. CHESTERTON

I am known to be . . . one that loves a cup of hot wine with not a drop of allaying Tiber in't.

WILLIAM SHAKESPEARE

No poems can please nor live long which are written by water drinkers. Ever since Bacchus enrolled poets, as half-crazed, amongst his Satyrs and Fauns, the sweet Muses have usually smelt of wine in the morning.

HORACE

Had Neptune when first he took
    charge of the Sea,
Been as wise, or at least been as
    merry as we,

Away with you, Water, destroyer of wine.

CATULLUS

These traitorous thieves,
    accursed and unfair,
The vintners that put water in
    our wine.

FRANÇOIS VILLON

Wine has two defects: if you add water to it, you ruin it; if you do not add water, it ruins you.

SPANISH PROVERB

Water is the only drink for a wise man.

HENRY DAVID THOREAU

He'd have thought better on't
    and instead of his brine,
Would have filled the vast ocean
    with generous wine.

MR. POPELY

Wine and Health

Wine is the most beautiful and hygienic of beverages.
LOUIS PASTEUR

Why is wine so special? Partly because for most of its history, and mankind's, it has been his one source of comfort and courage, his only medicine and antiseptic, his one recourse to renew his tired spirits and lift him above his weary, saddened self. Wine was the foremost of luxuries to millennia of mankind.

HUGH JOHNSON

We drink one another's health and spoil our own.

JEROME K. JEROME

Wine is the most ancient dietary beverage and the most important medicinal agent in continuous use throughout the history of mankind.

SALVATORE P. LUCIA, M.D.

The best medicine is wine.

ALCAEUS

The dysentery is improving. The army is only slightly worse for it now. Wine is being distributed to the troops; it is the best preventative.

PERCY, A SOLDIER DURING
THE PRUSSIAN CAMPAIGN
OF 1807

Like my friend the Doctor, I have lived temperately, eating little animal food. . . . I double, however, the Doctor's glass and a half of wine, and then treble it with a friend; but halve its effects by drinking the weak wines only. The ardent wines I cannot drink . . . now retired . . . at the age of seventy-six.

THOMAS JEFFERSON

Of all drinks, wine is most profitable, of medicines, most pleasant, and of dainty viands, most harmless.

PLUTARCH

Wine is wonderfully suitable for man if in sickness, as in health, it is administered in fair and proper measure.

HIPPOCRATES

Wine is one of the noblest cordials in nature.

JOHN WESLEY

There are more old wine drinkers than old doctors.

GERMAN PROVERB

I think it is a great error to consider a heavy tax on wines as a tax on luxury. On the contrary, it is a tax on the health of our citizens.

THOMAS JEFFERSON

people who never drink wine, whether naive or doctrinaire, are fools or hypocrites?

CHARLES BAUDELAIRE

Penicillin may cure human beings, but it is wine that makes them happy.

SIR ALEXANDER FLEMING

As Plinie saith, wine so it be moderately used, is a thing ordeined of god. It doth quench the thirst, revive the spirites, comfort the hart, sharpen the wyt, gladdeth a doleful mind, maketh a good memorye, killeth yl humors, maketh good blood.

JOHN FLORIO

Let none at misfortune or losses
    repine,
But take a full dose of the juice
    of the vine;
Diseases and troubles are ne'er
    to be found,
But in the damned place where
    the glass goes not round.

THOMAS SHADWELL

If wine disappeared from human production, I believe there would be, in the health and intellect of the planet, a void, a deficiency far more terrible than all the excesses and deviations for which wine is made responsible. Is it not reasonable to suggest that

Wine gives strength to weary men.

HOMER

The unearned increment of my grandfather's Madeira.

JAMES RUSSELL LOWELL,
TO A FRIEND
COMMISERATING WITH HIM
ABOUT SUFFERING FROM
GOUT

Satisfy your hearts with food and wine, for therein is courage and strength.

HOMER

I have taken more out of alcohol than alcohol has taken of me.

WINSTON CHURCHILL

After bread comes wine, the second nutriment given by the Creator to sustain life and the first to be famed for its excellence.

OLIVIER DE SERRES

Alcohol is a depressant to check the mental exhilaration produced by extended sobriety.

ANONYMOUS

Chronic and inescapable sobriety is a most horrible affliction.

ALDOUS HUXLEY

Drink slowly
Only men in rags
And gluttons old in sin
Mistake themselves for carpet
    bags
And pour their wine straight in.

GEORGE H. BOYNTON SR.

Place a substantial meal before a tired man, and he will eat with effort and be a little better for it at first. Give him a glass of wine or brandy, and immediately he feels better—you see him come to life again before you.

ANTHELME BRILLAT-SAVARIN

Wine not only strengthens the natural heat but also clarifies turbid blood and opens the passages of the whole body. It strengthens also the members. And its goodness is not only revealed in the body but also in the soul, for it makes the soul merry and lets it forget sadness.

RUFUS OF EPHESUS

Drink a glass of wine after your soup, and you steal a ruble from the doctor.

RUSSIAN PROVERB

Wine keeps its happy patients
    free
From every painful malady;
Our best physician all the year;
Thus guarded, no disease we
    fear,
No troublesome disease of
    mind,

Until another year grows kind,
And loads again the fruitful
    vine,
And brings again our health—
    new wine.

ANACREON

Wine sloweth age, it strengtheneth youth, it helpeth digestion, it abandoneth melancholie, it relisheth the heart, it lighteneth the mind, it quickeneth the spirits, it keepeth and preserveth the head from whirling, the eyes from dazzling, the tongue from lisping, the mouth from snaffling, the teeth from chattering, and the throat from rattling; it keepeth the stomach from wambling, the heart from swelling, the hands from shivering, the sinews from shrinking, the veins from crumbling, the bones from aching, and the marrow from soaking.

ANONYMOUS, 13TH CENTURY

Wine . . . is a great increaser of
the vital spirits; it very greatly
comforteth a weak stomack,
helpeth concoction, distribution
and nutrition, mightily
strengtheneth the natural heat,
openeth obstruction, discusseth
windiness, taketh away sadness,
and other hurt of melancholy.

DR. TOBIAS VENNER

Take this, he said, and held aloft
A vine stock branching fair.
Heaven's noblest gift to human
    kind
Entrusted to thy care.
Go plant it on the sunny hills,
For health and length of days,
And press its fruit for joyous
    drinks
And the creator's praise.

ANONYMOUS

Humor

What contemptible scoundrel stole the cork from my lunch?

W. C. FIELDS

A good general rule is to state that the bouquet is better than the taste, and vice versa.

STEPHEN POTTER

I like best the wine drunk at the cost of others.

DIOGENES

What marriage is to morality, a properly conducted licensed liquor traffic is to sobriety.

MARK TWAIN

He talked with more claret than clarity.

SUSAN ERTZ

A heavy drinker was offered grapes at dessert. "No, thank you," he said, pushing the dish away from him. "I am not in the habit of taking my wine in the form of pills."

ANTHELME BRILLAT-SAVARIN

LADY AT DINNER PARTY: You mean to tell me that you never ever let water touch your lips? Then what do you use to clean your teeth, pray?
RETIRED MAJOR: An obscure white wine, Madam.

ANONYMOUS

The girls of Bordeaux, I'm afraid,
You would hardly consider as staid:
A young Bordelaise
Knows of dozens of ways
In which she can get bordelaide.

CYRIL RAY

Wine improves with age—I like it more the older I get.

ANONYMOUS

'Twas Noah who first planted the vine
And mended his Morals by drinking its wine.

BENJAMIN FRANKLIN

No, Agnes, a Bordeaux is not a house of ill repute.

GEORGE BAIN

The best use of bad wine is to drive away poor relations.

FRENCH PROVERB

There was a young lady at court
Who said to the King, with a
    snort:
"Was it humor or shyness
That prompted your Highness
To put Spanish Fly in my port?"

C. D. CUDMORE

Always dress in the color you are tasting.

JACQUELINE. L. QUILLEN

Champagne

Champagne: the great civilizer . . .
CHARLES-MAURICE DE TALLEYRAND

Come quickly, I am tasting stars!

> DOM PERIGNON, UPON FIRST TASTING CHAMPAGNE

Warm Dom is better than cold Bud.

> ANGELA F. BUNGER

But the monarch of all wines is Champagne. Ah, me! How it bubbles, how it sparkles, this most ravishing of all wines! It is at once the most enticing and the most exhilarating. It is genial, comforting, stimulating, irradiating and divine. It refreshes, regales, cheers and transports.

> MAJOR BENJAMIN CUMMINGS TRUMAN

Champagne: bottled sunlight.

> LORD THOMSON OF CARDINGTON

Champagne is one of the elegant extras of life.

> CHARLES DICKENS

No government could survive without champagne. Champagne in the throats of our diplomatic people is like oil in the wheels of an engine.

> JOSEPH DARGENT

In victory you deserve champagne; in defeat, you need it.

> NAPOLEON BONAPARTE

I drink it [champagne] when I'm happy and when I'm sad. Sometimes I drink it when I'm alone. When I have company, I consider it obligatory. I trifle with it if I'm not hungry and drink it when I am. Otherwise, I never touch it unless I'm thirsty.

> LILY BOLLINGER

I like it [champagne] because it always tastes as though my foot is asleep.

> ART BUCHWALD

Champagne, with its amber hue, its éclat, its sparkle and its perfume, arouses the senses and produces a cheerfulness which flashes through the company like a spark of electricity. At the magic word champagne, the guests, dull and torpid with good feeding, awake at once. This lively, ethereal and charming beverage sets in motion the spirits of all; the phlegmatic, the grave and the philosophic are surprised to find themselves amiable; in the wink of an eye (or the pop of a cork) the whole banquet has changed its physiognomy.

CHARLES BAUDELAIRE

No other wine produces an equal effect in increasing the success of a party, and a judicious Champagne-giver is sure to win the goodwill and respect even of those who can command it at pleasure.

THOMAS WALKER

And one can always be very careful if one just has a little glass of bubbly along with one's predicament.

ISAK DINESEN

The evaporation of a joyous day
Is like the last glass of Champagne, without
The foam which made its virgin
  bumper gay.

GEORGE GORDON, LORD
BYRON

Lulled in a nine years' sleep
A child of Dionysus here abides
Imprisoned in his keep
Of dark green glass with round
  and glassy sides,
The entrance stopped with a
  cork and metal cap
And muzzled like a dog with a
  cage of wire—
Grim skeleton bedizened in a
  wrap
Of golden foil like kingly shroud
  that hides
Disintegration in a proud attire.
But loose the wire, and, lo, the
  prisoned slave
Stretches his muscles, heaves at
  the tight-closed door,

Heaves yet again and, like the
   whispering wave
That bursts frost-sparkling on a
   summer shore,
Leaps out, a fount of foam;
   then, changed again,
Dissolves to liquid sunlight.
   Golden wine
Brims every glass. Seen through
   each crystal pane,
In tall straight jets or whirled in
   spiral twine
The hurrying air-beads to the
   surface strain,
An April shower of bright
   inverted rain.

MARTIN ARMSTRONG

I've tried, but it's always in vain
Not to drink so much champagne,
But when I'm in trouble
I do need that bubble
—and it happens again and
   again.

CYRIL RAY

If port is the wine of reflection,
champagne is the wine of whim
and spontaneity.

CLIFTON FADIMAN

When fortune frowns, and
   friends forsake,
And faith in love is dead—
When a man has nothing left to
   stake,
To hope, nor yet to dread—
One godlike pleasure doth
   remain,
Worth all the joys he's lost—
The glorious vintage of Cham-
   pagne,
From silver goblets tossed!

CHARLES TOVEY

Champagne is the only wine a
woman can drink and still
remain beautiful.

MADAME DE POMPADOUR

My only regret in life is that I
did not drink more champagne.

JOHN MAYNARD KEYNES

Gentlemen, in the little moment
that remains to us between the
crisis and the catastrophe, we
may as well drink a glass of
champagne.

PAUL CLAUDEL

Here's to champagne, the drink
divine
That makes us forget our
troubles;
It's made of a dollar's worth of
wine
And three dollars' worth of
bubbles.

ANONYMOUS

Champagne for my real friends
Real pain for my sham friends.

FRANCIS BACON

I think wealth has lost much of
its value if it has not the whim-
sical sallies of wit that are the
natural productions of Champagne.

SARAH FIELDING

You can have too much champagne to drink but you can
never have enough.

ELMER RICE

And we meet with Champagne
and chicken, at last.

LADY MARY ASHLEY
MONTAGUE

A man must not dream of dying
before he has drunk five thousand bottles of Champagne and
smoked a hundred thousand
cigars.

PRINCE OTTO VON
BISMARCK

A woman should never be seen
eating or drinking, unless it be
lobster salad and *champagne*.

GEORGE GORDON, LORD
BYRON

Champagne bubbles make the
heart grow fonder.

ANONYMOUS

Mistress-like, its brilliance vain,
Highly capricious and inane . . .

ALEXANDER PUSHKIN, WHO
DRANK CHAMPAGNE WITH
EVERYTHING

The most agreeable and (to me)
most pernicious of all alcoholic
liquids, champagne . . .

ARNOLD BENNETT

A single glass of champagne imparts a feeling of exhilaration. . . . A bottle produces the opposite effect.

WINSTON CHURCHILL

Champagne is the wine-lover's luxury.

JANCIS ROBINSON

A good party is where you enjoy good people, and they taste even better with champagne.

WILSON MIZNER

Nectar strained to finest gold,
Sweet as Love,
As virtue cold.

ANONYMOUS

Truth, they say, lies in a well,
Why, I vow I ne'er could see;
Let the water-drinkers tell,
There it always lay for me.
For when sparkling wine went round,
Never saw I falsehood's mask;
But still honest truth I found
In the bottom of each flask.

RICHARD BRINSLEY
SHERIDAN

Red wine for children, champagne for me, and brandy for soldiers.

PRINCE OTTO VON
BISMARCK

There is a glorious candor in an
honest quart of wine,
A certain inspiration which I
cannot well define.
How it bubbles, how it sparkles,
how its gurgling seems to
say:
"Come! on a tide of rapture let
me float your soul away!"

EUGENE FIELD

To the Mall and the Park
Where we love till 'tis dark,
Then sparkling Champaigne
Puts an end to their reign;
It quickly recovers
Poor Languishing lovers,
Makes us frolic and gay, and
drowns all sorrow.

SIR GEORGE ETHEREGE

... The advantages of giving champagne with whatever limit at the beginning of dinner are these: that it has the greatest relish, that its exhilarating quality serves to start the guests, after which they seldom flag and that it disposes people to take less of other wines after, which is a relative and sometimes even an absolute saving to the pocket of the host and it is undoubtedly a saving to the constitution of the guests.

THOMAS WALKER

They sigh, not from the heart,
 but from the brain,
Vapours of vanity and strong
 Champagne.

LADY MARY WORTLEY
MONTAGU

I was far from successful with
 Susie,
A highly imperious floosie,
Who said "try me again,
But with *proper* champagne,"
Because Susie's too choosy for
 Bouzy.

CYRIL RAY

Claret

*I find that nearly all my more knowledgeable wine-drinking
friends are claret men at heart.*

ROBIN DON

A great claret is the queen of all natural wines and . . . the highest perfection of all wines that have ever been made. It is delicate and harmonious beyond all others.

H. WARNER ALLEN

Red bordeaux is like the lawful wife; an excellent beverage that goes with every dish and enables one to enjoy one's food. But now and then, a man wants a change. . . .

FRANK HARRIS

How I like claret! . . . It fills one's mouth with a gushing freshness, then goes down cool and feverless; then, you do not feel it quarrelling with one's liver. No; 'tis rather a peace-maker, and lies as quiet as it did in the grape. Then it is as fragrant as the Queen Bee, and the more ethereal part mounts into the brain, not assaulting the cerebral compartments, like a bully looking for his trull . . . but rather walks like Aladdin about his enchanted palace, so gently that you do not feel his step.

JOHN KEATS

[The magnum of 1864 Chateau Lafite] was like passing from fine prose to the inspiration of poetry.

H. WARNER ALLEN

One never tires of summer sunsets; they are always beautiful and yet they never are quite the same . . . That is also the secret of the appeal which Claret has for all wine lovers; it is the most perfectly balanced wine and in ever a new garb; harmony without monotony.

ANDRE L. SIMON

Gude claret best keeps out the
     cauld,
And drives away the winter
     soon;
It makes a man baith gash and
     bauld
And heaves his soul beyond the
     moon.

ALLAN RAMSAY

Claret is the liquor for boys; port for men; but he who aspires to be a hero must drink brandy.

SAMUEL JOHNSON

There is more flavour, more variety and more distinction about claret; it is a more interesting wine than Burgundy; a violin compared with a trumpet, a baritone as against a bass; but then some prefer basses.

EDMUND PENNING ROSWELL

To compare the magnificent harmony of a fine Bordeaux to a flight of alexandrines is to pay it a doubtful compliment . . . for the genius of no great wine is less emphatic, declamatory or monotonous. Grandeur it has, and in high degree, but I find the 'scansion' of Bordeaux, if scansion there must be, ranges from the Horatian to the Miltonic, from the rippling lyrics of Herrick to the sway and surge of Swinburne in the infinite variety of its scope; the 'rhythm' of its

incarnadine burden, the lilt of splendid majesty, never the din of rant drowning the creaking of the buskins. . . .

MORTON SHAND

It is wonderful what joy there is in excess. I stood it better today than yesterday. I came home not drunk though I had about two bottles of claret.

JAMES BOSWELL

Claret breedeth good humours, and is very good for young men with hot stomachs, but is hurtful for all that are of cold and moist constitution. To rheumy people, it is of all wines most pernicious.

DR. TOBIAS VENNER

What brain can fitly shape
A song to praise this grape,
Ranked over hill and plain
In lands about Bordeaux
Where the three rivers flow
To join the Atlantic main?
Praise first the great Chateaux
Lafite, Latour, Margaux,
Then two scarce less than
    these—
Haut-Brion and Ausone,
Then all those names well
    known
Of wines of all degrees.

    MARTIN ARMSTRONG

Its [Chateau Margaux 1871]
magic bouquet envelopes the
senses in a cloud of airy fragrance, scented like the breezes
from the Islands of the Blest, a
dream of grace and delicacy, the
twinkling feet of dancing
nymphs set free in our tedious
world. Its subtle symphony of
ever-varied shades of beauty
partakes of the poetry of speed,
of the perfect lines that form
and break and form again as
dancers weave an agile pattern.

    H. WARNER ALLEN

He who aspires to be a serious
wine drinker must drink claret.

    SAMUEL JOHNSON

Bacchus, god of mortal pleasure,
Ever give me of thy treasure.
How I long for t'other quart,
Ring and call the drowsy waiter
Hither since it is no later,
Why should good companions
part?

Whip a shilling he that's willing,
Follow this example round.
If you'd wear a lib'ral spirit,
Put about the generous claret,
After death no smiling's found.

    GEORGE FREDERIC HANDEL

I have never managed to like white Burgundy, though some of its humbler cousins from the Loire, especially Sancerre, please me greatly; the limitless world of German wine would take several score lifetimes to explore properly, but I have been doing what I can in thirty-odd years of my present span; though I will often seek an excuse to order red Burgundy (O that Richebourg, and my youth, long ago!). In the end I will always turn to claret, the noblest family in the great people of wine.

BERNARD LEVIN

Burgundy and Rhone

*Burgundy [is] . . . the soul and greatest common
measure of all the kindly wines of the earth.*

CHARLES EDWARD MONTAGUE

And when I depart from the earth to appear before my beloved Lord to account for my sins, which have been scarlet, I shall say to Him: "I cannot remember the name of the village. I do not even recollect the name of the girl, but the wine, my God, was Chambertin."

HILAIRE BELLOC

There are . . . certain geographical boundaries in the land of literature, and you may judge tolerably well of an author's popularity by the wine his bookseller gives him. An author crosses the port line about the third edition, and gets into claret; and when he has reached the sixth or seventh, he may revel in champagne and burgundy.

WASHINGTON IRVING

Burgundy for kings, champagne for duchesses, and claret for gentlemen.

FRENCH PROVERB

Nothing makes the future look so rosy as to contemplate it through a glass of Chambertin.

NAPOLEON BONAPARTE

Montrachet should be drunk on the knees with the head bared.

ALEXANDER DUMAS

The magistrate, asked whether he preferred claret or burgundy, answered: "This is a case, madam, in which it is so pleasant to examine the evidence that I always reserve my judgement for another week."

ANTHELME BRILLAT-SAVARIN

If Claret is the queen of natural wines, Burgundy is the king.

GEORGE SAINTSBURY

I serve your Beaune to all my friends, but your Volnay I keep for myself.

FRANÇOIS VOLTAIRE

It's a naive domestic Burgundy without any breeding, but I think you'll be amused by its presumption.

JAMES THURBER

To Burgundy:
Hail, Burgundy, thou juice
    divine
Inspirer of my song: —
The praises given to other wine
To thee alone belong.
Of poignant wit and rosy
    charms,
Thou can'st the power improve,
Care of its sting thy balm dis-
    arms,
Thou noblest gift of Jove!

INSCRIPTION TO THE
MUSICAL SOCIETY AT THE
FIVE BELLS TAVERN IN THE
STRAND

On my way to this town
[Beaune] I passed the stretch of
the Côte d'Or, which, covered
with a mellow autumn haze,
with the sunshine shimmering
through, looked indeed like a
golden slope. One regards with
a kind of awe the region in
which the famous crus of Burgundy (Vougeot, Chambertin,
Nuits, Beaune) are, I was going
to say, manufactured. *Adieu
paniers; vendanges sont faites!*
The vintage was over; the
shrunken russet fibres alone
clung to their ugly stick. The
horizon on the left of the road

had a charm, however; there is
something picturesque in the
big, comfortable shoulders of
the Côte.

HENRY JAMES

Burgundy has great genius. It
does wonders within its period;
it does all except to keep up in
the race; it is short lived. An
aged Burgundy runs with a
beardless Port. I cherish the
fancy that Port speaks the sentences of wisdom. Burgundy
sings the inspired ode. Or put it,
that Port is the Homeric hexam-
eter, Burgundy the Pindaric
dithyramb. . . . Pindar astounds.
But his elder brings us the more
sustaining cup. One is a foun-
tain of prodigious ascent. One is
the unsounded purple sea of
marching billows.

GEORGE MEREDITH

At the age of twenty, I believed
the first duty of wine was to be
red, the second that it should be
Burgundy. During forty years, I
have lost faith in much, but not
in that. . . .

ALEC WAUGH

The Bordeaux enlivens, the Burgundy invigorates; stronger drink only inflames; and where a bottle of good Beaune only causes a man to feel a certain manly warmth of benevolence—a glow something like that produced by sunshine and gentle exercise—a bottle of Chambertin will set all your frame in a fever, swell the extremities, and cause the pulses to throb.

WILLIAM MAKEPEACE THACKERAY

My grateful glass is lifted to the fine
Scholar who, when he found a precious wine,
Conveyed his sense of the supremely good,
Bringing it where it could be understood.
Having the best that Burgundy could send,
He gave it to no ordinary friend:
For one whose bounty spreads like gracious air,
The scholar found pure joy, a joy to share,
And, to make sure 'twas all that he could think it,
Companionably came and helped to drink it.
Long may such academic courtesies
Flourish; no fear that they should cease to please:
The scholar's gift to all that Christmas lent
A bouquet of the Chambertin he sent.

A PROVOST OF TRINITY COLLEGE

Wine, according to its quality and the soil where it was grown, is a necessary tonic, a luxury, and a fitting tribute to good food. And is it not also a source of nourishment in itself? Yes, those were the days, when a few true natives of my Burgundy village, gathered around a flagon swathed in dust and spiders' webs, kissing the tips of their fingers from their lips, exclaimed—already—"a nectar!"

COLETTE

Sweetbreads financiere and a bottle of mature Montrachet are not to be eschewed. But when I sit down to a plain daube of lamb and a bottle of Côtes du Rhone, I know that God's in his heaven, and all's right with the world.

GERALD ASHER

Even those who have forty years' old Port in their cellars had much better drink it. But my Hermitage [of 1846, drunk in 1886] showed not the slightest mark or presage of enfeeblement. It was . . . not a delicate wine. . . . But it was the manliest French wine I ever drank; and age had softened and polished all that might have been rough in the manliness of its youth.

GEORGE SAINTSBURY

Port

All wine would be port if it could.
PORTUGUESE PROVERB

If there is such a thing as a philosopher's wine, I think it may well be port. It has weight and dignity, calling for the concentrated mind. It is an evening, even a midnight, wine.

CLIFTON FADIMAN

Sip your spirits and cure your cold, but I will take port that will cure all things, even a bad character. For there was never a port drinker who lacked friends to speak for him.

WILLIAM MAKEPEACE THACKERAY

Women still regard port as their natural enemy.

AUBERON WAUGH

Port strengthens as it gladdens as no other wine can do.

GEORGE SAINTSBURY

Port is essentially the wine of philosophical contemplation.

H. WARNER ALLEN

Port—still the milk of don-hood.

GEORGE SAINTSBURY

Senatorial Port! we say. We cannot say that of any other wine. Port is deep-sea deep. It is in its flavour deep; mark the difference. It is like a classic tragedy, organic in conception. . . . Port speaks in sentences of wisdom.

GEORGE MEREDITH

The gentleman did take a drop
   too much
(Tho' there are many such)
And took more Port
Than was exactly portable.

THOMAS HOOD

When rectors drank Port Wine,
When no man talked of grace,
What jolly days were those!
Ah! then a parson's face
Displayed a parson's nose,—
A parson's nose of red,
Which gloriously did shine,
Supremely strong of head,
When rectors drank Port
   Wine. . . .

VERSES FROM *PUNCH*, AN 1870'S ENGLISH HUMOR MAGAZINE

The gentle fair on nervous tea
   relied,
Champagne the courtier drinks,
   the spleen to chase,
The colonel Burgundy, and Port
   his Grace . . .

GEORGE CRABBE

A pint of old Port and a devilled
biscuit can hurt no man.

R. S. SURTESS

In Vintage Port of noble year
What multifarious joys
   appear—
A liquid ruby; a bouquet
Like odours of a tropic day,
So ripe you'd almost say it glows
In the portals of the nose:
A palate luscious yet serene,
The right essential Hippocrene,
Blandness combined with
   potency;
A finish dry, but not too dry,
With just a hint of cedarwood
To spice the ripe fruit's nec-
   tarous blood.

MARTIN ARMSTRONG

Go and fetch a pint of port
But let it not be such as that
You set before chance-comers,
But such whose father grape
   grew fat
On Lusitanian summers.

ALFRED LORD TENNYSON

The gem of the three was a '73,
which had been allowed to
remain in wood till it was eight
or nine years old, and in bottle
for about as much longer before
I bought it. It had lost very little
colour and not much body of
the best kind; but if there ever
was any devil in its soul, that
soul had thoroughly exorcised
the intruder and replaced him
with an angel.

GEORGE SAINTSBURY

To taste port is to taste a tiny
atom of England and her past.

CLIFTON FADIMAN

It must appear strange to those who have always considered Port as the only wine suited for 'John Bull' and his climate, to learn how it was forced into use, only a century and a half ago. . . . Although exceedingly fine when originally of a good vintage and of sufficient age, it may justly be objected that owing to the large portion of Brandy added even to the best . . . the wine is rendered so powerful, that none but Englishmen can drink it.

THOMAS GEORGE SHAW

For Port . . . is incomparable when good. It is not a wine-of-all-work like Sherry. . . . It has not the almost feminine grace and charm of Claret; the transcendental qualities of Burgundy and Madeira; the immediate inspiration of Champagne. . . . But it strengthens while it gladdens as no other wine can do; and there is something about it which must have been created in pre-established harmony with the best English character.

GEORGE SAINTSBURY

No wine is worthy to be drunk in a highly civilized community which is not made of grapes alone, carefully selected from vines upon which practised labour has bestowed the proper culture. . . . It would almost seem as though the Portuguese made their wine as a vehicle for disposing of their brandy. . . . [N]o valid excuse has ever been made for the practise of adding such a quantity of brandy to the wines of Oporto. . . . The brandy is bad, distilled from figs and raisins of which no other use could be made.

C. REDDING, QUOTED BY
ALEC WAUGH

Though Port should have age,
Yet I don't think it sage
To entomb it as some connoisseurs do,
Till it's losing its flavor, and body, and hue;
I question if keeping it does much good
After ten years in the bottle and three in the wood.

R. H. BARHAM, QUOTED BY
ALEC WAUGH

Sherry

*Sherry is the brightest jewel in the vinous crown
of Spain. There is no wine like it.*

ANDRE L. SIMON

Sacke is the life and soul and spirit of man, the fire which Prometheus stole, not from Jove's kitchen, but his wine-cellar, to increase the native heat and radical moisture, without which we are but drousie dust and dead clay. This is nectar, the very nepenthe the gods were drunk with: 'tis this that gave Gannymede beauty, Hebe youth, to Jove his heavens and eternity. Do you think Aristotle ever drank sherry? or Plato cyder? Do you think Alexander had ever conquered the world if he had been sober? He knew the force and valour of sacke; that it was the best armour, the best encouragement, and that none could be a commander that was not double drunk with wine and ambition.

THOMAS RANDOLPH

If I had a thousand sons, the first human principle I would teach them should be, to for-swear thin potations and to addict themselves to sack.

WILLIAM SHAKESPEARE

All drinks stand cap in hand,
In presence of old Sherry.
Then let us drink old Sack, old
    Sack, boys,
Which makes us blithe and
    merry.

PASQUIL

We care not for money, riches,
    or wealth;
Old sack is our money, old sack
    is our wealth.

THOMAS RANDOLPH

The knot of hearty friendship
 Is by good sack combined,
They love no jars, nor mortal
    wars,
 That are to sack inclined;
Nor can he be dishonest,
 Whom sack and sugar feedeth,
For all men see, he's fat and
    free,
 And no ill humour breedeth:
Then let us drink old sack, old
    sack, boys,
 That makes us fat and merry,
The life of mirth, and the joy of
    earth,
 Is a cup of good old Sherry!

ANONYMOUS

It was golden in colour, suave and yet virile, as if a breeze of the sea had swept the grape and the ghost of its tang still clung and mingled with the bloom.

WYNDHAM LEWIS

Drink deep: this cup be preg-
    nant; and the wine
Spirit of wit, to make us all
    divine,
That big with sack and mirth we
    may retyre
Possessors of more soules, and
    nobler fire;
And by the influxe of this
    painted skie,
And labour'd formes, to higher
    matters flye;
So, if a nap shall take us, we
    shall all,
 After full cups have dreames
    poeticall.
Let's laugh now and the pres't
    grape drinke,
 Till the drowsie day-starre
    winke.
And in our merry, mad mirth
    run
Faster and further than the sun.

ANONYMOUS

Pale Sherry at a funeral, golden at a wedding, brown at any time . . . one man's Sherry is another man's poison. . . . Let your humour and your Sherry both be "dry."

CHARLES TOVEY

Sherry is a self-willed wine which gives a good deal of trouble to its guardians during its early years: it must have its own way, but, like many a diffi-cult child, when Sherry reaches the age of sweet reasonableness, it is the most amenable of all wines, the only one that will not let its nose be put out by being left overnight and even for some days in a decanter; the only one to put up cheerfully with ciga-rette smoke and over-scented women.

ANDRE L. SIMON

A good sherris-sack hath a twofold operation in it; it ascends me into the brains; dries me there all the foolish, and dull and crudy vapors which environ it, make it apprehensive, quick, inventive, full of nimble, fiery and delectable shape, which delivered o'er to the tongue which is the birth, becomes excellent wit. The second property of your excellent sherris is the warming of the blood, which before cold and settled left the liver white and pale, which is the badge of pusillanimity and cowardice, but the sherris warms it and makes it course from the inwards to the parts extreme. It illumineth the face, which as a beacon, gives warning to all the rest of this little kingdom, man, to arm, and then the vital commoners and inland petty spirits muster me all to their captain, the heart; who, great and puffed up with this retinue, doth any deed of courage, and this valor comes of sherris.

WILLIAM SHAKESPEARE

Toasts

To wine; kings it makes gods, and
Meaner creatures, kings.

WILLIAM SHAKESPEARE

Wine, one sip of this will bathe
the drooping spirits in delight
beyond the bliss of dreams. Be
wise and taste.

JOHN MILTON

Let love and wine their rights
  maintain,
And their united pleasures
  reign,
While Bacchus' treasures crown
  the board,
We'll sing the joys that both
  afford.

JOHN DYER

The house of hope is built on
  sand,
And life's foundations rest on
  air;
Then come, give wine into my
  hand,
That we may make an end of
  care.

HAFIZ

Drink, for you know not
  When you come, nor why,
Drink, for you know not why
You go, nor whence.

OMAR KHAYYÁM

Love and wine are the bonds
  that fasten us all,
The world but for these to
  confusion would fall,
Were it not for the pleasures of
  love and good wine,
Mankind, for each trifle their
  lives would resign;
They'd not value dull life nor
  could live without thinking,
Nor would kings rule the world
  but for love and good
  drinking.

TOAST OF 1675

Drink! Why wait for lamps? The
  day
Has not another inch to fall.
Fetch the biggest beakers—they
Hang on pegs on the wall.

GREEK VERSE, HIGHAM
BOWRA TRANSLATION

Then a smile, and a glass, and a
  toast, and a cheer
For all the good wine and we
  have some of it here.

OLIVER WENDELL HOLMES

There's many a toast I'd like to say
If only I could think it.
So fill your glass to Anything
And thank the Lord, I'll drink it!

WALLACE IRWIN

What is this life you are so sure about?
A flame that kindles, flashes, and goes out,
The unchanging heaven and the eternal sea
Serve but to mock our mutability.
And you before this wine who hesitate
For what, I ask you frankly, do you wait?

LI PO

Let other mortals vainly wear
A tedious life in anxious care;
Let the ambitious toil and think;
Let states or empires swim or sink;
My sole ambition is to drink.

HENRY CAREY

Day and night my thoughts incline
To the blandishments of wine,
Jars were made to drain, I think;
Wine, I know, was made to drink.

R. H. STODDARD

God in his goodness sent the grapes
To cheer both great and small;
Little fools will drink too much
And great fools none at all.

ANONYMOUS

O thou the drink of gods, and angels! Wine!

ROBERT HERRICK

Then let the goblet gleam for me, my friend
Pour forth care-soothing wine ere pleasures end.

PALLADAS

None but wine and true friendship are lasting and sure,
From jealousy free, and from
   envy secure;
Then fill all the glasses until
   they run o'er,
A friend and good wine are the
   charms we adore.

DRINKING SONG

Good company, good wine,
good welcome, make good
people.

WILLIAM SHAKESPEARE

Wine comes in at the mouth,
And love comes in at the eye,
That's all we know for truth,
Before we grow old and die.
I lift the glass to my mouth,
I look at you, and I sigh.

W. B. YEATS

Love his troth may soon dis-
   sever,—
Wine gives all, and gives forever.

GEORGE STERLING

I lift this cup
   To one made up
Of loveliness alone
   A lady of her gentle sex
The seeming paragon,
   Her health
And would on earth
   There stood more of like
      frame
Then life would be all poetry
   And weariness a name.

CHARLES COTESWORTH
PINCKNEY

To Celia
Drink to me only with thine
   eyes
 And I will pledge with mine;
Or leave a kiss but in the cup,
 And I'll not look for wine.

BEN JONSON

To the corkscrew—a useful key
to unlock the storehouse of wit,
the treasury of laughter, the
front door of fellowship, and the
gate of pleasant folly.

W. E. P. FRENCH

Let us drink and be merry,
    dance, joke, and rejoice
With claret and sherry, theorbo*
    and voice,
The changeable world to our Joy
    is unjust,
All treasures uncertain, then
    down with your dust.
 In frolic dispose your pounds,
    shillings, and pence
 For we shall be nothing a hun-
    dred years hence.

    THOMAS JORDAN

Leave the flurry
To the masses;
Take good wine
And fill your glasses.

    GEORGE H. BOYNTON SR.

Let wine's praise be sounded,
Healths to topers all
    propounded;
We shall never be confounded,
 Toping for eternity!
Pray we: here be thou still
    flowing,
Plenty on our board bestowing,
While with jocund voice we're
    showing
 How we serve thee—Jubilee!

    LATIN SONG

Come, love and health to all:
Then I'll sit down.
Give me some wine, fill full,
I drink to the general joy
O' the whole table.

    WILLIAM SHAKESPEARE

Now then, the songs; but first
    more wine.
The gods be with you, friends of
    mine!

    EUGENE FIELD

Here's to mine and here's to
    thine!
 Now's the time to clink it!
Here's a flagon of old wine,
 And here we are to drink it.

    RICHARD HOVEY

While there's life on the lips,
 while there's warmth in the
    wine;
One deep health do I pledge,
 and that health shall be thine.

    OWEN MEREDITH

*a twelfth-century stringed instrument

Light the candles and pour the red wine into your glass. Before you begin to eat, raise your glass in honor of yourself. The company is the best you'll ever have.

DAVID HALPERN

May our love be like good wine: grow sweeter as it grows older.

OLD ENGLISH TOAST

Fill up your cup, but spill not
   the wine
If you so do, it is an ill sign.

ROBERT HERRICK

This bottle's the sun of our
   table,
His beams are rosy wine;
We planets that are not able
Without his help to shine.

RICHARD BRINSLEY
SHERIDAN

Then fill the cup, fill high! fill
   high!
   Nor spare the rosy wine.
If death be in the cup, we'll
   die—
     Such death would be divine.

JAMES RUSSELL LOWELL

Fill every beaker up, my men,
pour forth the cheering wine:
There's life and strength in every
drop—thanksgiving to the vine!

ALBERT GORTON GREENE

Here's to the maiden of bashful
   fifteen
Here's to the widow of fifty;
Here's to the flaunting, extrava-
   gant queen
And here's to the housewife
   that's thrifty.
Let the toast pass—
Drink to the lass;
I'll warrant she'll prove an
   excuse for the glass.

RICHARD BRINSLEY
SHERIDAN

Comrades, pour the wine
   tonight
For the parting is with dawn;
Oh, the clink of cups together,
With daylight coming on!

RICHARD HOVEY

He who clinks his cup with
   wine
Adds a glory to the wine.

GEORGE STERLING

To our host:
The rapturous, wild and ineffable pleasure of drinking at somebody else's expense.

HENRY SAMBROOKE LEIGH

May you have many children
and may they grow as mature in taste
and healthy in color
and as sought after
as the contents of this glass.

IRISH PROVERB

To exalt, enthrone, establish and defend,
To welcome home mankind's mysterious friend:
Wine, true begetter of all arts that be;
Wine, privilege of the completely free;
Wine the recorder; wine the sagely strong;
Wine, bright avenger of sly-dealing wrong,
Awake, Ausonian Muse, and sing the vineyard song!

HILAIRE BELLOC

Here's to wine
  It accentuates the curves
    And negates the brakes.

GEORGE H. BOYNTON SR.

Here's to the good time I must have had.

ANONYMOUS

Wine gives a kind of release from care
And courage to subdue the fair;
Instructs the cheerful to advance
Harmonious in the sprightly dance
Hail! goblet rich with generous wines!

ANACREON

Here's to us that are here, to you that are there, and the rest of us everywhere.

RUDYARD KIPLING

Say why did Time,
His glass sublime
Fill up with sands unsightly,
When wine he knew,
Runs brisker through,
And sparkles far more brightly.

THOMAS MOORE

Burgundy's juice is red as blood
 That warms a maiden's veins;
And clear as amber from the
   flood
 The yellow wines of Spain;
Pure and bright as summer
   showers
 The vintage of the Rhine,
The drops of Bordeaux's purple
   bowers
 Fit for the Gods! Divine!
But Oh! these sparkling drops of
   bliss
 From vine-crowned towers of
   Rheims,
That touch my lips like a
   woman's kiss
 And light my heart like flames!
That sparkle like the laughing
   light
 Of Aphrodite's eye,
And thrill me with their sweet
   delight
 I love thee—"Extra Dry."

MAJOR MAGINNIS

Observe, when Mother Earth is
   dry
She drinks the droppings of the
   sky,
And then the dewy cordial gives
To every thirsty plant that lives.
The vapors which at evening
   weep
Are beverage to the swelling
   deep;
And when the rosy sun appears
He drinks the ocean's misty
   tears.
The moon too quaffs her paly
   stream
Of lustre from the solar beam.
Then hence with all your sober
   thinking!
Since Nature's holy law is
   drinking,
I'll make the law of Nature
   mine,
And pledge the Universe in
   wine.

THOMAS MOORE

May we never want for wine,
nor for a friend to help drink it.

ANONYMOUS

Drink to-day, and drown all
    sorrow,
You shall perhaps not do it to-
    morrow:
Best, while you have it, use your
    breath;
There is no drinking after death.

Wine works the heart up, wakes
    the wit,
There is no cure 'gainst age but
    it:
It helps the headache, cough
    and tisic,
And is for all diseases physic.

Then let us swill, boys, for our
    health;
Who drinks well, loves the
    commonwealth.
And he that will to bed go sober
Falls with the leaf still in
    October.

JOHN FLETCHER

We meet 'neath the sounding
    rafter,
And the walls around are bare;
As they shout back our peals of
    laughter
It seems that the dead are there.
Then stand to your glasses,
    steady!
We drink to our comrades' eyes:
One cup to the dead already—
Hurrah for the next that dies!

Not here are the goblets
    glowing,
Not here is the vintage sweet;
'Tis cold, as our hearts are
    growing,
And dark as the doom we meet.
But stand to your glasses steady!
And soon shall our pulses rise:
A cup to the dead already—
Hurrah for the next that dies!

BARTHOLOMEW DOWLING

Some delight in fighting Fields,
Nobler transports Bacchus
    yields,
Fill the bowl I ever said, 'tis
    better to lie drunk than
    dead.

TOAST OF 1766

Here's to the heart that fills as
the wine bottle empties.

ANONYMOUS

When Father Time swings
    round his scythe,
Entomb me 'neath the boun-
    teous vine,
So that its juices red and blythe,
May cheer these thirsty bones of
    mine.

EUGENE FIELD

Come, once more, a bumper!—
    then drink as you please,
Tho' who could fill half-way to
    toasts such as these?
Here's our next joyous
    meeting—and, oh, when we
    meet,
May our wine be as bright and
    our union as sweet!

THOMAS MOORE

For love and song
To the vine belong
To the vine, with its strength
    Titanic;
Small wonder it grows
Where the lava flows,
And the warm earth heaves
    volcanic.

From the East it came
With its warmth of flame,
And the Orient gave it fire;
They sang the vine
In Palestine
And they trod the grape at Tyre.

And prophet and seer
Of old Judea
With the wise of all the ages,
Have sung of wine
In strains divine,
From Papyrus to printed pages.

What was praised by them
Shall our lips condemn?
From such cant may the Lord
    deliver!
Let heart be merry,
God gave his berry,
And God is a careful giver!

JOSEPH DANA MILLER

The diamond sleeps within the
    mine,
The pearl beneath the water;
While Truth, more precious,
    dwells in wine,
The grape's own rosy daughter.

ANONYMOUS

Verities

*No thing more excellent nor more valuable than wine was
ever granted mankind by God.*

PLATO

Wine, dear boy, and truth.

ALCAEUS

(THIS FRAGMENT BECAME
THE PROVERB *IN VINO
VERITAS*, KNOWN TO BOTH
PLATO AND PLINY THE
ELDER.)

The wine-cup is the little silver
 well
Where truth, if truth there be,
 doth dwell.

WILLIAM SHAKESPEARE

Le vin nous enseigue le respect
et la vigne . . . la modestic.
(Wine teaches us respect and
the vine modesty.)

OLIVIER LEFLAIVE

One barrel of wine can work
more miracles than a church
full of saints.

ITALIAN PROVERB

Wine in itself is an excellent
thing.

POPE PIUS XII

If God forbade drinking, would
He have made wine so good?

CARDINAL RICHELIEU

Where Satan cannot go in
person, there he sends wine.

JEWISH PROVERB

Wine is wont to show the mind
of man.

THEOGNIS

Bacchus, n. A convenient deity
invented by the ancients as an
excuse for getting drunk.

AMBROSE BIERCE

Drink moderately, for drunkenness neither keeps a secret, nor
observes a promise.

MIGUÉL DE CERVANTES

Take counsel in wine, but
resolve afterwards in water.

BENJAMIN FRANKLIN

In wine negotiations,
Buy on bread, sell on cheese.

FRENCH PROVERB

There is no gladness without
wine.

THE TALMUD

Wine is only sweet to happy men.

JOHN KEATS

Wine softens a hard bed.

SPANISH PROVERB

Pure water is not sufficient to keep up the strength of working men.

COMTE DE BUFFON

Excellent wine generates enthusiasm. And whatever you do with enthusiasm is generally successful.

PHILLIPPE DE ROTHSCHILD

Who, after wine, talks of war's hardships or of poverty?

HORACE

A meal without wine is like a day without sunshine.

ANTHELME BRILLAT-SAVARIN

Wine is the intellectual part of a meal, meats are merely the material part.

ALEXANDER DUMAS

It is difficult to enjoy a good wine in a bad glass.

EVELYN WAUGH

There are no good wines, only good bottles.

FRENCH SAYING

There are all sorts of wine, young and old, good and bad, still and sparkling. There are times, moods and occasions when young wine will give us greater pleasure than the old; others when we shall enjoy the company of the old far more than that of the young.

ALEC WAUGH

Drink because you are happy, but never because you are miserable.

G. K. CHESTERTON

Of a brave man and a good wine, ask not whence they came.

GERMAN PROVERB

A person with increasing knowledge and sensory education may derive infinite enjoyment from wine.

ERNEST HEMINGWAY

Dead Lucre: burnt Ambition: Wine is best.

HILAIRE BELLOC

Wine is also a beauty spot on the cheek of intelligence.

OMAR KHAYYÁM

Nullam, Vare, sacra vite prius
    severis arborem.
(O Varus, plant no tree in pref-
    erence to the sacred vine.)

HORACE

Drink wine, and you will sleep
    well.
Sleep, and you will not sin.
Avoid sin, and you will be saved.
Ergo, drink wine and be saved.

MEDIEVAL GERMAN SAYING

The fine wine leaves you with something pleasant; the ordinary wine just leaves.

MAYNARD AMERINE

First the man takes a drink, then the drink takes a drink, then the drink takes the man.

JAPANESE PROVERB

Drinking wine makes such fools of people, and people are such fools to begin with, that it's compounding a felony.

ROBERT BENCHLEY

The very best of vineyards is the cellar.

GEORGE GORDON, LORD BYRON

Never think of leaving perfumes or wines to your heir. Administer these yourself, and let him have the money.

MARTIAL

Wine ever pays for his lodging.

GEORGE HERBERT

Man shall not live by bread alone.

MATT. 4:4

They are not long, the days of
    wine and roses;
Out of a misty dream
Our path emerges for awhile,
    then closes
Within a dream.

ERNEST DOWSON

Drink Wine, and live here
    blithefull, while ye may:
The morrow's life too late is,
    Live today.

ROBERT HERRICK

Let us eat and drink; for
tomorrow we shall die.

ISA. 22:13

Anyone who knows history . . .
must surely know his wines.

ARNOLD TOYNBEE

It is sometimes forgotten that
only one of the two peaks of
Parnassus was sacred to Apollo,
the other belonging to
Dionysus.

GEORGE SAINTSBURY

Wine is life.

PETRONIUS

Wine . . . is a food.

OLIVER WENDELL HOLMES

The best glass of white wine is
    the first,
The best glass of red is the last.

ANONYMOUS

If food is the body of good
living, wine is its soul.

CLIFTON FADIMAN

A bottle of good wine, like a
good act, shines ever in the
retrospect.

ROBERT LOUIS STEVENSON

Life is too short to drink bad
wine.

ANONYMOUS

No wine, no company; no wine,
no conversation.

CHINESE PROVERB

As long as we have wine, a pack
of cards, and a fire let anything
happen.

SPANISH PROVERB

Money spent taking care of good wine is money well spent.

FRENCH PROVERB

The rarest virtue that a single lady can possess—the virtue of putting wine on the table.

WILLIAM COLLINS

Wine is a bride who brings a great dowry to the man who woos her persistently and gracefully; she turns her back on a rough approach.

EVELYN WAUGH

Water separates the people of the world, wine unites them.

ANONYMOUS

Aliud vinum, aliud ebrietas. (Wine is one thing, drunkeness another.)

ROBERT BURTON

Wine is a remedy for the moroseness of old age.

PLATO

BIBLIOGRAPHY

Allen, H. Warner. *A Contemplation of Wine*. London: Michael Joseph, 1951.

———. *The Romance of Wine*. New York: Dover Publications, Inc., 1971.

Antrium, Minna Thomas, ed. *A Book of Toasts*. Philadelphia: Henry Altemus, 1902.

Belloc, Hilaire. *The Praise of Wine*. London: n.p., 1931.

Bespoloff, Alexis, ed. *The Fireside Book of Wine*. New York: Simon & Schuster, 1972.

———. *The New Frank Schoomaker Encyclopedia of Wine*. New York: William Morrow & Company, Inc., 1988 (rev.).

Blackburne, Robin. *Vintage Versage: A Collection of Rhymes, Parodies, and Wine Nonsense*. Hamilton, Bermuda: Balmoral, 1984.

Brillat-Savarin, Anthelme. *The Physiology of Taste*. trans. by M. F. K. Fisher, New York: Harcourt Brace, 1994.

Broadbent, Michael. *Complete Guide to Wine Tasting and Wine Cellars*. New York: Simon & Schuster, 1984.

———. *The Great Vintage Wine Book*. New York: Alfred A. Knopf, 1980.

———. *The Great Vintage Wine Book Vol 2*. London: Mitchell Beazley, 1992.

Brooks, Fred Emerson, ed. *Buttered Toasts.* Chicago: Forbes, 1911.

Carter, Everett. *Wine and Poetry.* Davis: University of California Library, 1976.

Chesterton, G. K. *Wine, Water, and Song.* 20th ed. London: Methuen, 1946.

Clotho, comp. *Prosit: A Book of Toasts.* San Francisco: Paul Elder, 1904.

Copeland, Lewis and Copeland, Faye. eds. *10,000 Jokes, Toasts, & Stories.* Garden City: Halcyon House, 1939.

The Concise Oxford Dictionary of Quotations. Oxford, England: Oxford University Press, 1960.

Coates, Clive. *Grand Wines: The Finest Chateaux of Bordeaux.* Berkeley: University of California Press, 1995.

Curtis, Charles P. Jr., and Ferris Greenslet. eds. *The Practical Cogitator.* Boston: Houghton Mifflin, 1950.

Daintich, John, ed. *Bloomsbury Treasury of Quotations.* London: Bloomsbury Publishing Plc., London, 1994.

Dick, William B., ed. *Dick's Book of Toasts, Speeches, and Responses.* Danbury: Behrens, 1883.

Dickson, Paul, ed. *Toasts.* New York: Crown Publishing, 1991.

Digby, Joan and John Digby, eds. *Inspired by Drink: An Anthology.* New York: William Morrow, 1988.

Doutrelant, Pierre-Marie. *Les Bons Vins et Les Autres.* Paris: Seuil, 1976.

Evans, Bergen, comp. *Dictionary of Quotations.* New York: Avenel Books, 1978.

Exley, Helen, ed. *Wine Quotations.* Watford, U.K.: Exley Publications, 1994.

Fadiman, Clifton, ed. *Dionysus: A Case of Vintage Tales About Wine.* New York: McGraw Hill, 1962.

Fadiman, Clifton and Sam Aaron. *The Joys of Wine.* New York: Henry M. Abrahams, 1975.

Flesch, Rudolf, ed. *The Book of Unusual Quotations.* New York: Harper & Row, 1957.

Foulkes, Christopher. *The Colour Atlas of Wine.* London: Segraves Foulkes Publishers and Malcolm Saunders Publishing Ltd., 1995.

Gabler, James M., ed. *Wine Into Words.* Baltimore: Bacchus, 1985. Garrison, Robert L., comp. *Here's To You!* New York: Crown, 1980.

Goodfellow, Adam, comp. and William Payne, ed. *A Book of Old Songs, Healths, Toasts, Sentiments, and Wise Sayings Pertinent to the Bond of Good Fellowship.* New York: New Amsterdam, 1901.

Gray, Arthur, ed. *Toasts and Tributes.* New York: Rhode & Hoskins, 1904.

Gross, John. *The Oxford Book of Aphorisms.* New York: Oxford University Press, 1983.

Grossman, Harold. *Guide to Wines, Spirits and Beers.* New York: Charles Scribner's Sons, (rev) 1964.

Henry, Lewis C., ed. *5000 Quotations.* Garden City, NJ: Garden City Books, 1952.

———. *Toasts for All Occasions.* Garden City: Garden City Books, 1949.

Johnson, Hugh. *The Story of Wine.* London: Mitchell Beazley, 1989.

———. *Vintage.* New York: Simon & Schuster, 1989.

Johnson, Hugh, Dora Jane Janson, and David Revere McFadden. *Wine: Celebration and Ceremony.* New York: Cooper-Hewitt Museum/The Smithsonian Institution's National Museum of Design, 1985.

Kaplan, Justin, ed. *Bartlett's Familiar Quotations.* Boston: Little Brown & Company, 1992.

Kearney, Paul W., ed. *Toasts and Anecdotes.* New York: Edward J. Clode, 1923.

Khayyám, Omar. *The Rubaiyat of Omar Khayyám.* Edward Fitzgerald, trans. New York: Crowell, 1879.

Koken, John M., comp. *Here's To It!* New York: Barnes, 1960.

Lausanne, Edith. *The Great Book of Wine.* New York: Galahad Books, 1970.

Lichine, Alexis. *Wines of France.* New York: Alfred A. Knopf, 1965 (4th ed. rev).

————. *Encyclopedia of Wines & Spirits.* New York: Alfred A. Knopf, 1969.

Lowe, Paul E., ed. *The Twentieth Century Book of Toasts.* Philadelphia: David McKay, n.d.

Matthews, Patrick, ed. *Christie's Wine Companion.* Topsfield: Salem House, 1987.

McNutt, Joni G. *In Praise of Wine.* Santa Barbara: Capra Press, 1993.

Mencken, H(enry). L(ouis). *A New Dictionary of Quotations on Historical Principles from Ancient and Modern Sources.* New York: Alfred A. Knopf, 1942.

Mosher, Marion Dix, comp. *More Toasts.* New York: Wilson, 1932.

Muir, Frank. *An Irreverent and Thoroughly Incomplete Social History of Almost Everything.* New York: Stein and Day, 1976.

Murphy, Edward F. *The Crown Treasury of Relevant Quotations.* New York: Crown Publishers, 1978.

The Oxford Dictionary of Quotations. London: Oxford University Press, 1954.

Parker, Robert E. *Place a Drop of Wine Near My Lips When I Die.* New York: Vantage, 1977.

Penning-Roswell, Edmund, ed. *Wines of Bordeaux.* New York: Scribners, (4th ed.) 1981.

Peter, Dr. Laurence, Jr. *Peter's Quotations, Ideas for Our Time.* New York: William Morrow & Co., 1977.

Price, Pamela Vandype. *Wine Lore, Legends and Traditions.* Middlesex: Hamlyn, 1985.

Ray, Cyril. *The Complete Imbiber.* Nos. 1–7, London: 1956–64.

———. *Lickerish Limericks.* London: J. M. Dent & Sons, Ltd., 1979.

Robinson, Jancis. *The Great Wine Book.* New York: William Morrow, 1982.

———. *Oxford Companion to Wine.* Oxford University Press, 1994.

———. *Tasting Pleasure.* New York: Viking, 1997.

———. *Vines, Grapes and Wines.* New York: Alfred A. Knopf, 1986.

Saintsbury, George. *Notes on a Cellar Book.* London: Macmillan, 1963.

Seldes, George. *The Great Quotations.* New York: Pocket Books, Simon & Schuster, Inc., 1984.

———. *The Great Thoughts.* New York: Ballantine Books, 1985.

Simon, Andre L. *A Dictionary of Wine.* New York: Longmans, Green & Co., 1936.

———. *The History of Champagne.* London: Octopus Books Limited, 1971.

———. *Wine in Shakespeare's Days and Shakespeare's Plays.* London: Curwen, 1964.

———. *Wines of the World.* London: McGraw-Hill Book Company, 1967.

Stevenson, Burton Egbert. *The Home Book of Quotations.* New York: Dodd, Mead & Company, 1934.

Stevenson, Burton, comp. *The Macmillan Book of Proverbs, Maxims, & Famous Phrases.* New York: Macmillan, 1948.

Taylor, Jennifer, ed. *The Wine Quotation Book.* London: Robert Hale, 1989.

Tripp, Rhoda Thomas, comp. *The International Thesaurus of Quotations.* New York: Harper & Row, 1970.

Waugh, Alec. *In Praise of Wine.* New York: William Morrow & Company, Inc. (3rd ed.), 1971.

Yoxall, H. W. *The Enjoyment of Wine.* London: Michael Joseph, 1972.

PHOTO CREDITS

Diane Ong, *Wine* (page 27 lower right), SuperStock

Claude Monet, *The Luncheon* (page 28 upper left), Stadelisches Institute of Art, Frankfurt, Germany/Bridgeman Art Library, London/SuperStock

The Wine Harvest, 16th century French tapestry (page 28 lower right), The Bettman Archive/CORBIS-Bettman

Frans Hals, *The Merry Lute Player* (page 61), Harold Samuel Collection; Corporation of London/SuperStock

Jacob Jordaens, *The King Drinks* (page 62 upper left), The Bettman Archive/CORBIS-Bettman

Nicolas Poussin, *Andrians*, also known as *The Great Bacchanal with Woman Playing a Lute* (page 62 lower right), Musee du Louvre, Paris/SuperStock

G. Cruikshanic, *Wine Tasting at the London Docks* (page 63 upper left), Library of Decorative Arts, Paris, France/Explorer, Paris/SuperStock

Henri Eugene Le Sidaner, *Le Café du Port* (page 63 lower right), Christie's Images/SuperStock

Pierre-Auguste Renoir, *The Luncheon of the Boating Party* (page 64 upper left), Phillips Collection, Washington, D.C./Giraudon, Paris/SuperStock

Claude Monet, *Luncheon on the Grass* (page 64 lower right), Musee d'Orsay, Paris/SuperStock

Edgar Degas, *In a Café (The Absinthe)* (page 65), Musee d'Orsay, Paris/SuperStock

Ernest Bieler, *Festival of the Wine Growers* (page 66 upper left), Explorer, Paris/SuperStock

Walter D. Sadler, *Testing the Vintage* (page 66 lower right), Christie's Images

Richard Emil Miller, *Café L'Avenue, Paris* (page 67 upper left), The Cummer Museum of Art and Gardens, Jacksonville/SuperStock

Eduard von Grutzner, *One Too Many* (page 67 lower right), Josef Mensing Gallery, Hamm-Rhynern, Germany/Bridgeman Art Library, London/SuperStock

Graham Knuttel, *Wine and Roses* (page 68 upper left), New Apollo Gallery, Dublin/SuperStock

Adam Woolfit, *18th Century Glasses* (page 68 lower right), CORBIS

INDEX